Thomas Keneally

Thomas Keneally began writing in 1964 and has published twenty-two novels since. They include *The Chant of Jimmie Blacksmith*, *Confederates* and *Gossip from the Forest*, each of which was shortlisted for the Booker Prize. In 1982 he won the Booker with *Schindler's Ark*, since made by Steven Spielburg into the internationally acclaimed film, *Schindler's List*. His novels *The Playmaker*, which was dramatised as the award-winning play *Our Country's Good*, and *Flying Hero Class* are also being filmed. He has also written several works of non-fiction, including *The Place Where Souls are Born* about the American Southwest. He is married with two daughters and lives in Sydney.

SCEPTRE

Also by Thomas Keneally and published by Sceptre

Homebush Boy

THOMAS KENEALLY

SCEPTRE

First published in 1995 by Hodder and Stoughton
A division of Hodder Headline PLC
A Sceptre Paperback

British Library Cataloguing in Publication Data

Keneally, Thomas
  Homebush Boy
  I. Title
  823 [F]

ISBN 0 340 64728 0

Printed and bound in Great Britain by
Cox and Wyman Ltd, Reading, Berkshire

Hodder and Stoughton
A division of Hodder Headline PLC
338 Euston Road
London NW1 3BH

To my valiant parents, who tolerated the GMH fanatic of 1952.

Glory be to God for dappled things—
For skies of couple-colour as a brinded cow

Gerard Manley Hopkins

'Where in God's name is Homebush?'

Max Harris, 1964

Homebush
Boy

I

Born in Sydney in the southern hemisphere's spring of
1935, after Mussolini had in another unimaginable continent invaded Ethiopia, and while my parents were down
from the country town of Kempsey trying their luck in
bad economic times, I had been named Michael Thomas
by my mother. But my father incorrectly registered me
under the name Thomas Michael. At home and in the
world my mother and father called me Michael. It suited
my nature to have an untouched and unsuspected legal
first name in reserve, though two-named possibilities did
not tease me at that stage nor need delay us here. For
this is not an exhaustive tale of boyhood but of the one
reckless, sweet, divinely hectic and subtly hormonal year.
That is, in my case, 1952. It seems to outweigh the other
years, to be the most succulent and the most dangerous.
Its consequences, lightly embarked on, have not to this
day ceased to tease, govern and turn on me.

At sixteen, I was in the business of defying gravity in
an unlikely place called Homebush. I think it might have
been named this because it had once been a tangle of
scrub not much more than fifteen miles west of Sydney
and encountered by nineteenth-century colonial gentry as
they rode west or came up the Parramatta River to their
country homes in Strathfield. By 1952 Homebush was a
lesser suburb of the remote Commonwealth of Australia
in the still existent British Empire.

In 1952 I did not smoke, and abhorred jovial adolescent
farting. I seemed even to myself barely to eat. I studied
both alone and with a blind friend, Matt Tierney.

I worked, ran races and did my best to be everywhere at once – an undiscriminating blob of European yearning.

I shared my aesthetic impulses in particular with a calmly anarchic boy called Mangan, angular, dreamy and stubborn, who lived in grander but not grand Strathfield. He had the goods over all of us and over his suburb: he intended to be a Trappist monk. Mangan had given a name to the axis he and I and a few other conscripted souls formed: the Celestials. I have always thought of us since under that title. We were a gang whose main act of subversion was to pretend we were not where we were.

At night, by the railway line in Homebush, I slept as lightly as the teenage eighteenth-century prodigy of poetry, Thomas Chatterton, whose work I had found in the Mitchell Library in Sydney. He was one of my heroes because he proved you could become immortal by seventeen years of age. At five years, said his biographer, Chatterton ordered a cup to be made with an angel blowing a trumpet, so that it might blow his name throughout the earth. And the angel did a great job, since Chatterton's poetry, much of it in 'bogus Middle English' and supposed to have been written by a medieval priest called Rowley, was hugely praised, even though people objected to the deception. When Chatterton took arsenic in London in 1770, Wordsworth called him 'the Marvellous Boy', and Keats dedicated *Endymion* to him.

> Arise, good youth, for Sacred Phoebus' sake!
> I know thine inmost bosom, and I feel
> A very brother's yearning for thee steal
> Into my own . . .

As I slept in the Eastern Australian nights of 1952, in Tennessee Elvis – soon to be discovered – was scowling and thrusting his way towards fame. Rock was imminent. But I went against the age, and Chatterton was my rocker. I too wanted to be a marvellous boy without having to take arsenic. I was a very strange little bugger.

Wafer-thin dreams occupied these nights by the railway embankment between Homebush and Flemington, the Western Line being only thirty yards from and level with my parents' bedroom window in our upstairs flat at No. 7. Sydney's umber electric trains passed east to town, and west to the Blue Mountains and the mulga, the bushweek towns in the great plains, from which came Australia's wealth -- wheat, beef, wool. The big 52 locomotives, such as my grandfather had driven, hauled the imports from the port of Sydney into that hinterland we called *the bush*. Accustomed pulsations from those New South Wales Government Railway's steam engines were barely felt in my Chatterton sleep. The railway line ran through our senses like a river, dragging memory and compartments full of lovers by our windows.

The railway had been the road of high drama for the four of us. My mother, father, little brother Johnny, me. Now having grown angelic and having read modern poetry, I had contempt for it. As I stood at the top of the outside stairs, the embankment ran across my vision like a gag on the imagination. But earlier, as an infant down from the country with my parents, I had been excited to see the traffic of electric and steam trains, had stood on the little castellated balcony of our upstairs flat just to watch.

During the Second World War sentimental Yanks (some of them, of course, Southerners) had been borne down that rail to training camps in the bush. When we waved, they showered us with two-bob coins, used comic books and gum. A silver rain of coin of the Realm and Wrigley's gum falling in Loftus Crescent.

Down the rail, too, went the guarded carriages of Italian POWs. Militia and regulars of Mussolini's Italian

Empire. They'd gone to a lot of trouble to prove the Australian 6th Division were supermen by surrendering to them in platoon, company, or battalion lots.

❊❊❊❊❊

The night my father, Leading Aircraftman Edmund Thomas Keneally, had gone to the Middle East, my pregnant mother and I had come down that line wistfully by electric train afterwards. I heard my mother tell someone later that my father harboured an ambition to move on to Europe during his foreign service in the Middle East (as from our position in the world's far south we dutifully called it). He might go to Ireland on leave and see his own emigrant father's village in north Cork. But the Japanese would soon come to preoccupy Australia's military and rule European service out.

As for us, Homebush was the one option. I can taste the flavour still of that extraordinary, fatherless Tuesday night, the blacked-out city, the special glow of dismal lights within the shuttered carriage, my grief for the warrior's leaving and my triumph in having my mother under my seven-year-old protection.

I woke at sundry times in the next three years feeling the first savage, gasping regret in my life, all to do with my father. At Auntie Kate's at Penrith one weekend, I'd said during an argument with him that I hoped he would be taken prisoner. Indeed his ship came close to being sunk by the Japanese in the Indian Ocean. He and other airmen slept on deck in life jackets as, in the radio hut, call after call from torpedoed vessels came in.

As male of the family, I gave my mother an anxious time. I would not be able to climb out of the lower half of my class. I was frequently incapacitated by asthma, which in those days mothers – not infections, the humid climate, the backyard grasses, the dust mites in

4

households – were blamed for. At five, in Kempsey, I had been admitted to hospital with a severe respiratory seizure which came close to taking my life. Then she would nurse me through pneumonia in 1944, and ended so exhausted the doctor put me in the Children's Hospital so that she could have a night's rest.

But despite these vulnerabilities, she invested me with the proud position of household male. I carried the napkin bag. I walked beside her to Mass. Our alliance was no doubt intensified by the absence of father and spouse. She had a preposterous faith in my survival and that I would succeed at school.

Then, when history had had its way, the railway by our windows delivered the soldiers home. First, a very spruce-looking Lance Corporal Frizzell, yellow from taking Atabrin for malaria. My father was still with a squadron in Egypt, but Laurie Frizzell had had to return only from the closer shores of New Guinea. He carried the rifle with which he'd made the Yellow Peril think twice, and was still gaitered in case he encountered swamps. An immaculate hero just stepped off the electric train. And towards him ran Dulcie Frizzell, a honey-blonde woman. Until that point, I'd thought of her as ancient – twenty-eight years, something like that. But I was astounded by her ardour. When alerted by neighbours she ran up the street and flung herself into Laurie's arms. A phenomenal kiss occurred, far more primal than anything I'd seen at the Vogue Cinema. All by courtesy of the steel river which had washed up Lance Corporal Frizzell.

From observing the kiss, it struck me at ten years that in some ways women were girls for a long time. This was a piece of information I would later temporarily forget when I became a Celestial.

One day in late 1945, we caught more or less the same train which had delivered Lance Corporal Frizzell. It was a case of my mother, myself, and my nearly three-year-old fair-haired brother going to collect my father from the war. Train first, then bus to a great barn of a hall at Bardwell Park. We were there by ten in the morning, the hall packed with young mothers waiting to show husbands the two or three or four-year-old fruit of the pre-embarkation leaves of 1941 or '42. And all the old children like me believed that the war had transformed their fathers to sages and heroes, that there would never be a quarrel with them as in the previous dull days before the old man went off to the cataclysm.

Men arrived from the ship all day, in some sort of order, alphabetical or otherwise, and two thousand reunions had taken place before a jovial middle-aged corporal told us that the Ks were coming, and we were taken out to meet a truck from which Sergeant K and other men jumped, each one with a kitbag and a suitcase, and there were extraordinary caresses and an unfamiliar paternal patting of my cheek. I had a sense of proudly surrendering care of the hearth back to him. Yet I felt odd with him, like many of the children of that era who greeted returning fathers. Later generations would receive this sense of hiatus on the way to adulthood through divorce. My generation got it through the wartime removal of the father. He embraced for the first time my handsome little blond brother, who reassured himself by saying, 'Daddy? Daddy?'

And then of course we all went home by train on the Western Line, the Western Line serving all drama, restoring paternity too.

But these days a Celestial, I would walk miles rather than catch a train. Mangan and I and sightless Matt Tierney, who listened to music with his chin lifted, and the Frawley girls caught the train in to the free Town Hall concerts of the Sydney Symphony Orchestra, conducted by a genius named Sir Eugene Goossens. But we would have flown there on the wings of desire if we could have.

I possessed a handy *belle dame sans merci* named Bernadette Curran, head prefect of Santa Sabina convent school in Strathfield, who sometimes joined us for those afternoon concerts. She was slim, athletic, and had olive, unmarred skin and a forthright manner. Occasionally I crossed her path, and this tale is in part an exorbitant log of these transits of Venus.

My Byronic friend Mangan and I walked rather than rode to school because we had become neo-Gothic children and needed time for reflection on how to deal with our placement in time and the universe.

Mangan was very happy that Trappist monks had come from France and England and settled outside Melbourne, thus making it possible for him to make his way back to the Middle Ages. The Trappists lived in utter silence.

'It'll be nothing *but* gesturing then, Mangan,' Larkin, a fringe though mocking Celestial, told him. Larkin was one with Mangan and me aesthetically, but he was also a solemnly self-declared agnostic. Even though he had to sit through Religion classes, brief as they might be at our senior level, he had frankly announced his state of mind to his parents. He made up for his heresies by his taste for poetry and history, and both he and Mangan were united in contempt for my own main heresy. Sporting passion. The ideal of the poet-athlete. 'No poet has ever worn shoulder-pads,' Mangan told me.

Those two and Matt had this over me: their relationship to the Western Line was in my eyes the right,

7

southern one, whereas I found myself improperly located on the north. The line's flinty, iron stench marred the dreams of incense. The old and by now clichéd story which I must try to tell as well as possible was this: the line separated me from the better suburb of Strathfield, from the older, more settled, hilly, leafy and genteel streets. As always in these situations, most of what I believed I loved and wanted was on the other side. Teachers and other boys said, 'You live down the other side of the line in Homebush, don't you?' So it was either in the school records or legible in my features. I was one street beyond the municipal pale.

I made up for it by dressing rakishly, as the Romantic poets had. If I could get away with it, and prefects generally could, I wore my blue-and-gold tie loose as a cravat. My grey felt hat was crushed. For Byron never did his hair. The seventeen-year-old prodigy Chatterton's shirt had been unbuttoned when he committed suicide. Percy Bysshe Shelley didn't wear neck ties. Within the limits of the grey serge uniform of St Patrick's Strathfield, I did my best to show people I was an aesthete and a wide-open spirit.

My father, who was a much more dapper person than I, saw through all the dishevelment I strained for. I heard him tell my mother that I was 'flash as bloody paint'. He groaned to see what I did to the school suit he went without beer to pay for. I *worked* on jamming the Oxford University Press Edition of the poet-hero-Jesuit Gerard Manley Hopkins (GMH to me) into my inside breast pocket, where both it and the fabric were forced weirdly out of shape. My mother was half-amused and thought it was other-worldliness, and that gave me hope that other women would too, particularly the Frawley girls, and above all of course Bernadette Curran of Strathfield, for whose sake all the perverse Chattertonian treatment I gave my clothes was designed. I believed Curran in particular needed to be captured by the sight of a suit pocket strained out of shape by the transcendent load it carried, the rectangular force of Hopkins' fierce, eccentric English.

> I caught this morning morning's minion, king-
> dom of daylight's dauphin, dapple-dawn-drawn
>   Falcon, in his riding
> Of the rolling level underneath him steady air . . .

In case the emanations of GMH didn't work on Curran, who was such a level kid, I spent a huge time making my auburn hair seem negligently done, fixing it then into Beethoven-esque licks with a gluey white preparation called Fix-a-Flex. My cowlick thus cemented could stand up against wind and rain, and remained in glued insouciance throughout an afternoon of English, History, Maths, Science, Rugby League practice and a long dawdle home with Matt Tierney, and Mangan the potential Trappist.

I went through all this brutalism of suit and hair not for the sake of a certain meeting, but on the off-chance of encountering the Frawleys and/or Curran in Meredith Street or elsewhere on the way back home. Mangan and I dawdling like a literary school beneath the box trees Strathfield Council lined its streets with; and handsome Matt listening sagely to us, and Larkin the sub-agnostic taking gentle shots at us. My most significant curl glued to the corner of the forehead, complementing Mangan's severely disordered tresses. Rose Frawley, the earthier of the two sisters, was always quick to say she thought Mangan and I were ratbags. But both of us thought that was just the girls' defence and that they all really *knew* that they were meeting serious presences. So when Rose Frawley asked, 'Haven't you finished reading that bloody book yet, Mick?' I thought it was just her way of dealing with the intensity of the Chattertonian and Hopkins-like splendour of Mangan and me.

Earth, sweet earth, sweet landscape, with leaves throng ...

Gerard Manley Hopkins, Society of Jesus. On his death bed he'd asked that all his poems be destroyed, and I imagined myself in that situation in a large, bees-waxed, cold room you could willingly slip away from into another state, and saying to crowds of Mangan-like peers, 'Burn all my poems, they were vanities.' Then when I had expired as lightly, fragrantly, crisply as biting into an Adora Cream Wafer, my literary executors would say, 'Not on your life. The stuff Mick wrote when he was sixteen, in particular *that* must live!'

Walking with or without Mangan on my way to collect Matt Tierney, I passed some big nineteenth-century houses located on the Strathfield side of the line. St Lucy's School for the Blind, Matt's earlier *alma mater*, was such a mansion, the home in the bush in Homebush-Strathfield for a family of nineteenth-century grandees called Meredith. One of the Meredith women had written a book on Victorian life in the Australian settlements. Of course it wasn't the sort of book I would ever write. We Celestials were too transcendent merely to report back colonial small talk.

From St Lucy's School for the Blind, when he was eight years old, Matt had engineered a remarkable escape with a friend. The two of them found out by intelligence – maybe one of the children who had not always been blind had told them – that you could be seen moving beyond the fence through the gaps in the palings, particularly if you had Matt's snow-white albino hair. So he and his accomplice had crawled a hundred yards on their hands and knees up Meredith Street to avoid being spotted from the school. Tussocks of grass, which always grew at the base of paling fences, screened them. Eyeless, they got as far as the Tierney house in Shortland Avenue, where Mrs Tierney had found them extracting coins with a knife out of Matt's money box.

I knew from this story, and from the way a smile took the corners of his mouth when Mangan and I were at our most rarefied, that Matt had plenty of go. He was stuck with us because he was in a sense our hostage. We were the ones who studied with him and read to him those books which were not yet in the Braille Library. He was, after all, a forerunner – the first blind child to attempt the Leaving Certificate – and the New South Wales Braille Library had not yet caught up with his needs.

He had the physique, the quickness of gesture, which would have made him a sportsman if he had been suddenly freed, and he would have hung around at least part of his time with the surreptitious smokers and beer drinkers and appreciators of 'women' (as they hopefully called the sixteen-year-olds from the Dominican Convent). But at least he was able to share with them and with me an athletic enthusiasm. And he had also the aforesaid advantage of living in Strathfield.

Amongst the occasional mansions were ordinary brick bungalows of the kind in which the unruly, un-punctual Mangans lived, in which the orderly Tierneys could be found, in which Bernadette Curran's parents raised their splendid daughters. The fragrant little gardens of these smaller houses were full of shrubs and flowers whose names I did not know but which did the service of bearing away the coaly, electric smell of the railway. At the height of summer, the Strathfield gardens looked desiccated and heat-frazzled, but they were as close as I could get to seasons of mists and mellow fruitfulness.

I was the sort of kid men took aside for serious talks. One was Mr Frawley, the Frawley girls' father. The other was Mr Aldo Crespi, who lived at Mrs Talbot's boarding house in the Crescent and who – everyone said – was her lover. He was an amnestied Italian prisoner of war who had escaped from a camp in the bush. He had found a place with Mrs Talbot who had fallen for his Italian palaver. Turning himself in at the end of the war, he returned to Italy and then re-emigrated to Australia to be with Mrs Talbot.

My father disapproved of Crespi and called him 'the Red Wog', since Mrs Talbot was a Leftist in the Strathfield Branch of the Labor Party and Aldo was her ideological sidekick. He had lived well with handsome though tubercular Mrs Talbot while – to quote my father – 'silly, bloody Australians' were off in foreign parts fighting the war he had abandoned.

I would sometimes meet Aldo as I walked up the hill in the Crescent, on the far side of the railway line. The Crescent was as straight as a die, and I'd see Aldo coming down the hill with his sample bag. He sold lotions and soaps and detergents door to door – my mother was one of his clients and said he 'really laid it on'. He seemed to make a good living since he was always so buoyant, a dapper little man. If he met me, he would put his sample bag down, because he had plenty to tell me.

'So you're going off to those bigots again?' he'd ask me. 'Those Franco-lovers who tell you to pray for poor Godless China? I tell you, China is better off under the Reds than it was under the warlords. Less than ten years ago, fifteen million Chinese were dying of famine. More than the population of this little country of ours. But that was okay with the bigots because the missionaries were still there.'

But sometimes he would be a residual Fascist. 'Those bigots will run down Mussolini while they praise Franco.

I tell you, if Mussolini hadn't been silly enough to put his money on Hitler, he'd still be in business, and Italy a much better place. Crikey, I'll give you the decent oil. Mussolini even treated political prisoners nicely. The world is bloody complicated, son, and they'll try to tell you, those bigots, that it's bloody simple.'

I could not ask him the questions I was really interested in. Had Mrs Talbot known he was the escaped enemy? And then the matter Mangan knew about somehow – that TB made people twice as sexual, destroyed their control. But it was hard to put *that* together with Mrs Talbot's severe good looks, and her pallor, and with how one day, as I was passing the boarding house at the top of the Crescent, which was not a crescent, I'd seen her put a handkerchief to her mouth and bring it away drenched with blood. There were mysteries to do with Crespi which superseded the mystery of how the Chinese were fed.

'Don't let them cross your wires,' he advised me. 'They have nothing better to do. My wires were crossed when I was a boy. First, the Church, then the Fascists. You think at first the one is the cure for the other. But they dance together. Look at the *industrial groupers* as they call themselves. The landscape of Fascism.'

'But surely you think that Stalin is a threat to Australia, Mr Crespi?' I asked him as always.

'Stalin is not as much a threat himself as what *they* will make of him. Besides, don't be fooled into thinking it's a choice between Stalin and the groupers. Between the inhuman and the inhuman, other choices can be made.'

I liked Crespi because the idea of galactic struggles between ideologies of good and evil suited my temperament. I suspected that even a pimple came from a struggle between the white deity of spirit and the dark one of flesh.

To my dialogues with Crespi I brought a selective sense of history. Some of the Brothers in my earlier

years at St Pat's talked a lot about the Spanish Civil
War, for in it the forces Crespi talked about had come
face to face. We were never told that the Republicans
had been a democratically elected government of Spain.
We were told, however, that they were nun-slayers and
priest-killers, and that in Madrid at the Alcazar, trusting
in the Virgin Mary, the garrison had held out for an
astounding time and been delivered at last by faith.

The other fellow who would take me aside and talk to
me as if I had a mission in the cosmic battle was wiry little
Mr Frawley, father of the Frawley kids, the two older
girls Rose and Denise, and two smaller boys about my
brother's age. Frawley was one of the industrial groupers
Crespi abominated. The groupers believed something like
this: Dr H. V. Evatt, leader of the Labor Party, a scholar,
a lawyer, first Secretary of the United Nations and a
former Cabinet Minister of the governments of Curtin
and of Chifley, was either too soft on Communism
of perhaps even a fellow traveller. The nexus between
the Labor Party – saviour of the working class and
guarantor of equities – and the Communist-controlled
unions was a scandal to men like Frawley. Look in
Doc Evatt's speeches and correspondence now, and you
will not find much to justify their broad fears. Poor
old Doc, who competed with the Conservative Prime
Minister Menzies to express fealty to the dying King
of England and the coming Queen! But to Mr Frawley,
either a dupe or a co-conspirator.

My father harboured the same suspicions and would
often utter them over the Sydney evening paper, the
Mirror. He did not become a grouper, however, an acti-
vist. The war seemed to have given him a certain cynicism
about joining things. Frank Frawley had been deprived of
his war and was fighting it here on the Western Line.

Frawley was a little wiry man like Crespi. He had
a cowlick and worked as a purchasing officer in the

New South Wales Government Railways, the crowd who with their brute locomotives ran their steel rail right through my sleep. He was a reader, and he too liked to believe in this struggle of dogmas at the end of time, and felt that 1952 was getting pretty late in the century and in history in general.

Mr Frawley's war was territorial, too. 'The Catholics founded the Labor Party,' he pronounced, 'and now we're being forced out of it by Reds.'

And he would say such things as, 'At least one classic Marxist objective is part of the platform of the Australian Labor Party. It's right there – *The Nationalization of all means of production, exchange and communication*. It lies there like a serpent at the heart of the party. And all of us told ourselves it didn't really matter. Mr Chifley said it didn't matter, Mr McGirr, Mr Cahill.'

Joe Cahill, the premier of the state, a good friend of Cardinal Gilroy's and a Papal Knight, escaped too much vilification from Mr Frawley though. No one believed he was Marxism's running dog. Besides, he was only a power at the state level. The Federal level, and above that the world and the universal level, were what interested Mr Frawley and me.

Some of the Brothers at St Pat's told us a lot about brave work undertaken by industrial groupers. The Communists intimidated union members and always insisted on an open ballot to intimidate them better. If that didn't work, we were told, the Reds then stole the ballot boxes for counting, and opened them in their own headquarters. The security of ballot boxes was one of the things the groupers fought for. There was a young man in Lewisham, a grouper who – Brother Markwell swore – had his arm broken with a cricket bat in a fight over a ballot box.

Mr Frawley couldn't take on Communism directly though. His office was not a Marxist breeding-ground, but was in fact full of members of the Knights of the Southern Cross, an Hibernian society, reliable men. There was little call for him to break his arm in his workplace defending ballot boxes. Instead, the occasional rough stuff Mr Frawley's band of groupers got involved in was aimed not against Reds but against the commandos of a rabid newspaper called *The Rock*.

The Rock was a very juicy scandal sheet edited by a man called Campbell. He did this on behalf of a fundamentalist group who were worried about Papism and its pomps and its decadence. It was so hugely popular, with its tales of pregnant nuns and buggering brothers, that people had to reserve it at Rossiter's newsagency on Parramatta Road to be sure of getting a copy when it came out on Tuesdays. It confirmed for Protestants all they had ever thought about the Whore of Babylon, but Monsignor Loane of St Martha's Strathfield had to exhort his own flock not to buy the rag since it only encouraged Campbell.

Early on, Campbell had excited his readers by telling them he intended to raid convents and liberate young nuns enslaved by Popish superstition and imprisoned in the cellars. To ward off Campbell, Mr Frawley served under the lieutenancy of a meat wholesaler called Kelleher, who lived in Homebush. Kelleher's corps of groupers would defend the convents from attack.

On the Western Line there were two places in particular which were susceptible to Campbell raids. One was St Anthony's Home for Fallen Girls at Ashbury, and the other was Lewisham Hospital, run by a company of genial nuns whose robes were sky blue and white. Both these convents had superb gardens, as if to fulfil the well-known dictum about flower beds and the Deity's heart. And nuns of both Orders had actually caught Campbell's scouts snooping around amongst the rhododendrons on reconnaissance.

In between serving as an undoubtedly brave convent sentry, Mr Frawley, whose parents like my father's were Irish emigrants, was a student of Ireland's grievances. He told me once, 'You have to suspect anyone called, say, Neill. They're probably descendants of Soupers. That's people who drop the O' from their name and abandoned their faith during the Famine in return for soup.'

I wondered why that didn't apply to Frawleys, if they'd all been O'Frawleys once. But I was almost manically polite, so I didn't force the issue.

In this way, during my journeys to and from the house of Matt Tierney, ground breaker, I would receive vigorous though intermittent and contradictory instruction on the nature of the world.

In that year of high circulation for the mad rag *The Rock*, I guiltily believed I'd met Campbell once. That had been three years before, in 1949, before *The Rock* became famous, before Campbell had brought what would now be called his 'tabloid' talents to it.

My mother was taking my brother and me back to Kempsey in New South Wales, where my maternal grandmother lived, on the North Coast Daylight. There had been a big good-looking man in a grey suit in our compartment. He'd worn his tie loosened and had an edge of danger. It was increased by the fact he got out and drank at each refreshment room at every station we stopped at. This wasn't uncommon on country trains in the late 1940s – men would jump off the train before it had stopped and run, suited and hatted and in the hope the beer was on, for the refreshment room. If it was, they would order three or four beers and drink them fast before the train left and come back to their seats meritoriously flushed and a little uncertain in speech.

Once, between Maitland and Taree, as I came back from the toilet, I saw the man from our compartment standing in the corridor with his face slackened. He was drinking from a flask he must have got filled at Maitland. He looked at me, first coldly and then with a good-natured derision. I was of course wearing my St Patrick's grey uniform, *Luceat Lux Vestra* on my breast pocket.

'The Brothers' boy,' he told me, as if it was a joke between us. He hadn't been like this with my mother. He'd been flirting with her, and every town we passed – Gosford, Wyong, Maitland, Merewether – he knew a story about, knew what the local economy was like, knew what houses were worth and what was the rent for shops. Whether it was worth owing a milkbar in Wingham. He'd quoted cousins and friends he had everywhere. I knew my mother considered him a pain, a blowhard. But out here in the corridor, I knew he wasn't going to tell me anything about the cost of housing, or how the timber mill at Dungog was going.

'You had your first hard one yet, sonny?' he asked.

I wasn't exactly a Celestial then, but I was on my way to being one, and am abashed to have to admit I had only the dimmest idea of what he meant. An erection, for certain. But something else as well? I was unworldly, and proud of it, so I said nothing.

'I've got a brother-in-law. A bit straight-laced. Doesn't smoke, drink. He has a paper. *The Rock*. Ever heard of *The Rock*?'

'No.'

'Well, that's bloody understandable. They ought to smarten themselves up. What they write about mostly is the evils of drink. To most Australians, the only evil with drink is we don't have enough. But stories, too, about the evils of the Church of Rome.'

He uttered this sentence lightly, as if he didn't really believe it himself. 'They ought to concentrate on that more. People like reading that. I could give you money for a good story. For example, do the Brothers sit you on their laps? Do they unbutton you? Things like that?'

'Nothing like that happens,' I said.

In primary school, one of the Brothers would sometimes sit boys on his lap, not surreptitiously, but in front of the lot of us. Classrooms operated from the desire to be noticed and favoured by the teacher, but this was a mark of favour I never envied. I didn't understand the reason for this behaviour though. A few knowing boys sniggered about it. Most of us were not knowing. The unease I felt when I saw it, the itchy, bilious sense – that was my business. It wasn't the business of this joker with the loose tie. This fellow who was one kind of smart-alec with me and another with my mother.

'If you had any stories like that, I could give you ten bob a pop. I've got a telephone number.'

He took out a card and gave it to me. 'Better put it away somewhere. Careful your mum doesn't find that when she's ironing your suit.'

What he didn't know was how well the Dominican nuns first and then the Brothers had prepared me for this hour. They had prepared me, in fact, for Satan in an Akubra hat to torture me, to offer me martyrdom. This fellow was a stupid man not to understand that. Ten bob wasn't even a temptation. It was an anti-climax. It was – though I didn't know the word then, and wouldn't until three years later when I came under the influence of literary Brother McGahan – *bathos*.

'See, I'm just going to Lismore to visit my wife. She's not too keen on me.' He winked. As if I had women trouble too. 'Then I'll be back at Sydney, that number. You could be my agent in the field. How would you like that?'

He extended his hand, but I didn't take it even though I was scared of him. We made our separate ways back to the compartment, and he returned to being the flash know-all all the way from Dungog to the small hamlet of Kundabung. Here we began to gather our luggage. My mother drenched a handkerchief from the solid glass water carafe in its silver plated bracket on the wall, *NSWGR* (New South Wales Government Railways) frosted on the surface of the bottle, and began the last tidying up of my brother's face, and combing of his hair. She wanted to show her parents in Kempsey that she had sparkling boys.

The man, whose name was not on the card I had been given – it said only *The Rock*, and had a telephone number – insisted on jovially carrying our ports to the door of the train and setting them down on the station. Emanations of conspiracy still came off him, I thought, aimed at me. But they evaporated when I saw my grandfather's face bearing down on us. The man did not try to make a friend of my grandfather or impress him with any information about dairy farming in the Macleay. He got straight back on the train and it was the last I saw of him.

I never told anyone I'd had this brush with possible Campbell. Later, I was fascinated to read in my father's copy of *Truth* – very much a secret activity with me, though I could manage to do it if I went to a different Mass from my parents – that Campbell's wife in the bush was angry with him because he was unfaithful and had used a horse whip on her. *The Rock* said that she had been bribed by the Knights of the Southern Cross and by the Vatican to say these things. And he, the man on the North Coast Daylight who had carried our bags, was the general against whom Mr Frawley stood as a brave NCO of Christ.

II

At the age of thirteen, Matt Tierney had come to St Pat's Strathfield with some fanfare. He possessed the aforesaid uniqueness of being the first blind boy in any state of the Commonwealth of Australia to attempt the Leaving Certificate. His markedly handsome features were utterly albino. His mother had suffered rubella when she was pregnant with him, and he'd been born with her features but with snow-white hair and skin and withered orbs of eyes. He had never seen anything, though he once told me his marred optic nerves were sensitive to gradations of light.

For the first four years of his high school, he had had for his guide a loud, eccentric, hectically generous boy called Martin Dahdah, who came from a Lebanese family. It seemed that nearly everyone in Australia up to the end of the Second World War had names which came from the British Isles, but there was a Lebanese draper or haberdasher in every town, and one family of Greeks, and one of Italians.

The year before, turbulent Dahdah had astonished everyone by going off to the minor seminary in Springwood in the Blue Mountains to do his Leaving Certificate and then begin studying for the priesthood, and so Matt didn't have a study companion any more. I wanted to be associated with Matt, who shone like alabaster and who appealed to some streak of what may have been both kindliness and passion for spacious gestures in me.

How to be fair to the sixteen-year-old Celestial and GMH lover who took over from Dahdah the Arab?

Amongst my other motives, noble and base, was athletic ambition too, which always ran high in me. I had seen Dahdah running with Matt on St Pat's oval, Matt with his head on his side as he followed the rattling of Braille type-pieces which Dahdah carried in a Nugget Boot Polish tin in his right hand. I was faster than Dahdah, and I thought of using two boot polish cans full of Braille pieces – twice the noise for Matt to follow. I could tell that Matt was a fast man too, a natural sportsman. We would do well together. If we practised enough, Matt would be able to run the bends of the oval at full pace. The fact that this athletic endeavour would be seen by Bernadette Curran gave it greater, not lesser worth.

Anyhow, in the January of 1952, with the glow of his vocation on his forehead, Dahdah had come to my place and asked me to be Matt's companion. We may have used the callow term 'take over Matt'.

I accepted the task up front and then tried to reconcile my parents to it. Other boys were more wary about taking Matt on as a study companion. This *was*, after all, the Leaving Certificate year, and university scholarships lay at the end, and it was hard enough to drag yourself through the process without also – this was the way many saw it – dragging someone else through as well.

The decision to become Matt's companion worried my parents too. Again, the sacrifices they made so that my brother and I could go to the Brothers, whose record with university scholarships stood so high, seemed imperilled. My father went without drink. My mother, who was by everyone's account a beautiful woman, had to line her holed shoes with newspaper. They gave up fashion and exuberance and social events, entertaining and being entertained, in the hope my brother and I would become doctors or lawyers. And I was close to being their first success. A minor academic star.

They were concerned about all the extraneous work I would have to do with the admired Matt. For example, he did Ancient History and I didn't. Yet I would need to read the Ancient History texts to him by the hour.

They were also probably more aware than I was that Matt was no neutral quantity, but a robust soul in his own right. That disease which turned Matt milk-white in his mother's womb and left him without any of the mechanisms of sight, would all his life threaten to make him appear less of a person, and like most blind people he would fight that belittling impulse in others, and only in the end come to a sort of truce with it.

Matt, who could have been anything if not for that untoward case of measles! In coming to St Pat's and studying amongst the sighted, he may have been a pioneer, but the sentimentality and ignorance of the age cast him as a curiosity and a freak. The *Daily Mirror* came and took a picture of Matt amongst the sighted boys, sitting at his desk, punching away at the Braille typewriter, a machine in which he rolled heavy pages of brown-grey paper. He punched keys with Braille characters on them, and indentations matching the keys appeared on the pages, so he could read what Brothers Adams or Harding or Markwell had said.

Few observers mentioned the armies of blind children for whom Matt stood. Few asked what was being done for them. They were safe in their institutions. They were securely enclosed at St Lucy's, named after a blind saint who'd found the light.

I was of course too young, too crass, too innocent not to be part of the general view that Matt was in part a hero and in part a freak. But if you were his friend, he proved to you daily that he was no more or no less than another boy. I slowly came to perceive too his parents' courage in letting him go forth amongst us ordinary Western Suburbs boys.

But they had family traditions of bravery. They came from South Coast farming families. Mr Tierney was an older man and had served in World War I. One of the fixtures in his living room was Bean's *History of Australia in the War of 1914–18*. He would sometimes point out the picture of the Cathedral of Albert in Flanders. Either the Germans or the British – I forget which – had put a charge in the spire and set it off, so that the Virgin who stood on top should no longer act as an aiming marker. The Virgin, therefore, leaned down at a crazy angle, reaching her infant towards the passing troops, perhaps inviting their mercy. I supposed that's what the Tierneys were doing. Lowering their child in the direction of the rough soldiery of St Pat's.

Mr Tierney told me one day while I was waiting for Matt and filling in time by looking at the photographs in Bean, about how he'd been wounded in the side near Amiens in the spring of 1918, and the wound had turned septicaemic in the military hospital. The army surgeons had tried everything, and in the end they had used boiling mercury, pouring it into the wound to cauterize it. Gentle Mr Tierney shook his head and smiled and said how much it had hurt – he had, in fact, fainted. He recounted this as if it were a story against himself, as if there were tougher blokes who wouldn't have passed out.

Subsequently, he'd worked on the Harbour Bridge during the Depression, and one day at the northern end had fallen off and survived, landing in what is now parkland near Milson's Point. Mr Tierney had – to use a term common amongst Civil War veterans in America – seen the elephant more than once. And now he lived in quiet Shortland Avenue where the brick villas were hunched down behind their dusty roses, and he went to a job somewhat like Mr Frawley's and showed none of the hubris I would have if my wounds had been cleaned out with boiling mercury on a great battlefield.

The Tierneys were brave when I turned up with a cemented cowlick and my unreliable smile and said, 'Gidday, Mrs Tierney, I'm Mick Keneally, and Alex asked if I'd see Matt to school and study with him.'

What did such a neat woman think of my deliberately bashed and battered felt hat, my suit distorted by the copy of Gerard Manley Hopkins in the breast pocket? And Matt came up the hallway with his long, white hands held out before him, and his questing smile.

'Gidday, Mick. Just hang on a sec. I'll get my bag.'

Like any teenager, he'd sometimes be abrupt with his mother.

'Where's my Breasted's *Ancient History*? Well, why *didn't* you put it back?'

These reproofs would usually be muttered. The smile would turn faintly testy if she fussed over his appearance. He'd brushed his own hair and tied his own tie, and didn't like it if she tried to straighten anything.

When his tussle with his mother ended, we were off up Shortland and into Francis Street. The corner of the oval in sight, where later in the year we would show our style with the Nugget tins full of braille type.

❀❀❀

This was an age of the hugest innocence, and therefore, of casual malice. Italians had begun to arrive in numbers, and Balts of every stripe – Lithuanian, Estonian, Latvian – and Poles and Greeks, but they had not yet changed the Australian equation. They were bundles of strange clothing on the edge of our vision. Britishness prevailed, and even the Irish-Australian working class were part of that Britishness. We stood for *God Save the Queen* in the cinemas. The part of Britain we most resembled might have been Belfast or Liverpool or Glasgow, a sun-struck version of any of those, of their demographics, their assumptions, their fervours and their clannish rivalries. The world had not quite yet opened our window, though there were some remarkable-looking strangers beginning to appear in the frame.

And in that sealed, antipodean room, to go along with all the other odd opinions, were some odd opinions about the blind. Mrs Tierney, who was tall – Matt had her face and her lankiness – was offended that some people looked upon the blindness of the child as a punishment of the mother. Since emigration to Australia was often from the poorer parts of the British Isles, folk superstitions arrived and sometimes pooled here. But then there were those who considered Matt too awesome a phenomenon to talk to directly. Outside St Dominic's Flemington on Sunday morning, women who had just addressed the unutterable Deity would say to Mrs Tierney, 'His shoe laces are undone.'

She would say, 'You can tell him yourself, if you like. He's quite intelligent. He's doing the Leaving Certificate.'

But people would scutter away. Mrs Tierney's lifetime mission was to educate the rest of us. To vanquish in all of us that primitive voice that said somehow that Matt was cursed and that the curse was contagious.

The school Matt and Mangan (on some mornings) and I approached through those quiet streets planted with box trees stood on a low hill either side of Edgar Street, Strathfield. Its buildings were topped by stumpy concrete Celtic crosses to indicate the origins of the Order. I would later find that buildings like the older of the school's two structures, the part where I'd begun as a third grader, attending the Christian Brothers on soldier's pay in the third last year of the war, were clones of Christian Brothers' buildings the world over.

Years later, I would visit one drear Irish afternoon the founding house of the Order in Waterford, and find its nineteenth and early twentieth-century buildings were like prototypes of Strathfield. Both empires, the British and the Irish, knew what architecture was appropriate to them. So you had august British court houses in the bush, to match the august, plum-red brick convents.

The Christian Brothers, like the best generals, preferred hills, and St Pat's was strung out on one flank of a hill they called Mount St Mary's.

To me, the line of school buildings seemed in some ways a defence against the haze of ennui which hung over the pleasant gardens, the brick bungalows, and the Federation-style meekness of the suburb of Strathfield, preferable though it might be to Homebush. Mangan and I were united in a purpose to redeem these streets by astounding and as yet unselected acts. One of them for me, however, was to work with Matt until he became amongst the sighted world the athlete he already was by nature.

Mangan had no crass sporting ambitions though, so he was the Celestial of Celestials. He and I appropriately were both doing Honours English and Honours History.

This year had given us a new version of History. We had, until now, believed that history had ended with the Federation of Australia on the First of January, 1901. But suddenly, there were all these books, given us by Brother Dinny McGahan from a press normally kept locked at the back of Fifth Year Blue's classroom, which dealt with the twentieth century. The twentieth century, the hem of whose garment Australia had touched at places like Gallipoli and Pozières, on the Kokoda Trail and at El Alamein! Brother McGahan had made me wonder about my father, who had spent those years keeping the Empire's ground either side of the Suez

Canal. Did my father know about the Lateran Treaty between Mussolini and the Vatican? Did he know about the *Anschluss*, and the Brenner Pass? The two beasts of Fascism and Communism ground the century with their hooves. But, my God, how dramatic!

These were aspects of history worthy of discussion by Celestials such as Mangan and I, and by Matt and occasionally by the very scholarly Dan Larkin whom Dinny McGahan described as 'a natural historian'. We would discuss 1930s appeasement on the way up the hill, or go through Pass History stuff like the unification of Italy say with Matt. When we uttered dates, Matt would repeat them, searching out with his white stick the kerb or the cracks in the paving. 'Yes, now. 1864, Garibaldi captures Naples.'

The 414 bus would usually come grinding up the road, green and yellow. It operated from Homebush to Strathfield by way of that well-paved hinterland. My little brother was on it, snappy in his lovingly tended grey uniform. He had my father's liking for dapperness and shiny shoes, and he was a sensible kid, and good at all the things I wasn't – maths and sciences. He didn't need long walks through quiet streets to gear himself up for greatness.

'There's your brother, Keneals,' other little buggers in short pants and laundered blue shirts would call out to him, and I would pretend not to notice too closely.

I had the renown of being Matt's offsider and was one of the school's minor athletes too. Though nothing like Peter McInnes from our class, an athlete known Australia-wide. John Treloar, the Australian 100-yard champion, has said Peter would be the greatest Australian Olympic sprinter. 1956, said Treloar, when the Olympics might be held in Melbourne . . . look out for McInnes. No question that Peter would be the first member of Fifth Year Blue to slide into fame. Even if I were to publish something brilliant early, Peter would already be a member of the national sprinting team.

I imagined being there in Melbourne, perhaps in the company of the lovely Curran. And as Peter wins the 100-metre Gold Medal, breaking records set by Jessie Owens, he jogs as Olympic athletes will to the front seat of the stadium to thank his closest advisers. Myself amongst them. The chief being Brother McGahan who, as well as introducing us to the *Anschluss* in Honours History, was also our running coach.

Though I wasn't an athlete-hero like Peter McInnes, through running with Matt, I might become a *moral* hero. A *moral* hero was something I yearned to be. Early in the year I'd taken to describing everyone in my Shakespeare essays as a moral hero, even at one stage applying the label to Horatio in Hamlet. Brother McGahan asked me nasally, 'Why do you call everyone a moral hero, Mick?'

The answer was, because of a hunger for grandeur, which Homebush and the Western Line could not slake. Mangan, too, had such a hunger.

'We are troubadours,' he'd told me one night two or three years before, when such a statement had sounded not banal but full of extraordinary fragrance. 'Travelling poets looking for a true home.'

Though he would have been embarrassed to talk in such ordinary images, these days the idea of what he had said ran between us like a charter.

Everyone else seemed to us awfully pleased with their time, their location. Even Matt, our hostage, retained a sneaking regard for the present and the suburbs. Mangan and I wanted to move in stranger darknesses.

'There's your brother, Keneals,' the fifth graders yelled.

Advancing from the direction of Matt's place, we came to the oval first. According to Brother Digger Crichton who had always taught woodwork at St Pat's, in the Brothers' first years here, during the Depression, people had lived in cardboard shanties in the paddock which was now the oval. 'How lucky you are boys . . .'

Crich Crichton had been a digger in World War I, and as a dispatch rider, had seen the Red Baron shot down. These days he attended every school Rugby League match and wrote a summary of it in beautiful calligraphy, signed *Cas Obs*. Casual observer.

The building of the oval, I realize now, must have been a sizeable effort, for on three sides retaining walls had to be thrown up to contain it. The place of sport as a human delight and as a moulder of souls. Only the bravest and most inept, like Mangan, stood aside from this enthusiasm. I dreamed of the poet-athlete. I would have admired GMH more – not less – if as well as writing his sprung rhythm English verse he had represented England in Rugby or cricket.

Mangan dared to look upon the oval as a wasted space. Whereas I had and would always have a fascination for well-tended green arenas surrounded by seats. I had been running here since I was eight, and had always wanted to run faster than I could manage, a desire Mangan had never once felt.

'I ask you,' he said once, 'what time did Napoleon run the 100 yards in? What time did Beethoven do for the 880 yards?'

On the oval the previous May, I had on one of my rare days scored a weaving try from a long way out against De La Salle, Ashfield. At such instants, you perform beyond your known limits. A divinity runs in you. *Cas Obs* had praised the performance on the school notice board.

Cricket was the one grand sport of the oval on which I could make no impact. Brother Dinny McGahan was often in the cricket nets with the First Eleven in the mornings. He was himself a stylish batsman. One of his training techniques which showed up the distance between myself and those gifted boys was that he would set up a gymnastic springboard, the kind you would put in front of a vaulting horse. On the far side of it he would line the First Eleven in the ring, and he would hurl the ball at the springboard. The ball would ricochet off like an edged shot from an uncertain but forceful batsman. The First Eleven, all only seven or eight paces from the springboard, had an instant to react when the big six-stitcher sprang off the board at an unexpected angle and came to them. Dinny McGahan was determined that everyone in his team would be fit to field in slips, the premier in-close positions behind the batsman. I would not have seen what they were seeing and catching.

Soon these boys cricketers would be in the two end rooms of the new building, doing Physics with Brother Buster Clare or Latin with Dinny. Writing clearly and without pain. Whereas even in dropping the catches they were taking, I would have been stung on the palm or wrist by that hornet of a red, hard ball. Or the catch would have caught me on my finger tips and brought all the blood up into the nails.

In the mornings prefects were supposed to supervise all the youngsters at the assembly in the front of the palisaded toilets and dressing rooms which we called the Stockade. But Dinny McGahan had taken me aside and told me not to worry about that. Just to settle in with Matt, in the end room, where we sat in adjoining desks around the middle of the middle row. Matt could set up the Braille typewriter, and we could cram a bit. Particularly learning our Robert's *Modern History*, which Brother Buster Clare had us recite by rote.

Buster Clare, responsible for half our success in the Leaving Certificate, was a very different man from Brother McGahan. He was large and muscular with a grizzled head, and in another life might have been a very forceful cop. His soutane was older and had less black in it than Dinny's and didn't fit him as well. Maybe he'd inherited it from a Brother who had died. The sash, which the more demonstrative brothers sometimes raised and held in their left hand as they spoke, looked very small in proportion to Buster's rugged body.

His pedagogic methods were simple: you had to recite the text off by heart for Buster. No extra marks for reading a biography of Napoleon or Metternich in your free time if you didn't get Robert's right down to the last preposition. And if you didn't, he would come down and ironically call you *mavourneen* (which I believe means *darling* in Gaelic) and declare you a fool and cuff your ear.

He would say too, 'I don't think we'll do the Second Empire this year. It was on the last two Leaving exams in a row.'

He loved this gambling on what would be *on*. He would say, 'I tipped twelve questions from the last Leaving Cert, *mavourneen*. So you just learn it the way I tell you, and then perhaps you won't end up shovelling sand for Strathfield Council as you deserve.'

Of course, you could play Pass History that way. But you needed the urbanity of Dinny McGahan to get through Honours History.

When we told the Frawley girls and Bernadette Curran about the way Brother Buster Clare ran his Pass History classes, they thought it was all pretty strange. The Dominican nuns who taught them weren't punters and wouldn't skip the Second Empire no matter how often it had been on the paper recently.

'It's all part of an education,' La Belle Curran told us once when she was at the Frawleys. She said it matter-of-factly, not with airs. She seemed to me to have no airs at all, and to be calm in all circumstances. My job was to evince some huge response from her. How to get it was connected to the pyrotechnics of GMH which I carried around over my heart.

Once we were all at our desks in Fifth Year Blue, we started the day with Dinny McGahan's Pass English. The New South Wales curriculum, *Silas Marner*, the fairly wimpy *Richard II*, a monarch so studiedly hapless that even Mangan and I, as much as we wanted to, found it hard to identify with him. And then Romantic poets.

St Agnes' Eve – Ah, bitter chill it was!
The owl, for all his feathers, was a-cold;
The hare limp'd trembling through the frozen grass,
And silent was the flock in woolly fold.

Hardly an indication in Pass English that there were twentieth-century novels, or that letters had in any way taken root in Australia. That news lay like a secret between the Honours English boys, Larkin, Mangan and Keneally, and Brother Dinny McGahan. Matt Tierney of course was in on the secret too, from listening to Mangan and me rave on about T.S. Eliot and *Murder in the Cathedral* and Graham Greene's *Brighton Rock* and GMH. I'm sure Dinny McGahan said extra prayers for us each morning, having exposed us to the theological doubt of Graham Greene's novels, and to the secularism of Eliot and Auden.

At twenty to ten, Dinny and Buster would switch rooms with each other. Buster would come in to our room, Fifth Year Blue, the room devoted more to the Humanities than Fifth Year Gold, whose strong suit was Maths and the Sciences. Under Buster, we Physics Pass and Maths Pass boys were the primitives now. Since we believed more in other things, including the thirteenth century, the greatest of all, the century of the troubadours, Mangan and I had cut ourselves off from half the glory and drama of our own century by eschewing Maths I and Maths II and doing the Sciences cursorily. We didn't see the Honours Physics Buster taught next door to his select body of students as in any way connected with the giant facts of the world anyhow, with the awful atomic wonders Joe Stalin meant to bring down on our heads.

I was aware that Matt certainly had the gifts for Honours this and Honours that. Honours was good to do because it gave you automatic stature as a *brain*. Matt had the capacity to be a brain whether in the Arts or the Sciences. But the Braille library didn't have the books for him yet. They didn't even have *Silas Marner* in Braille. He was the first blind boy ever to need *Silas Marner* and *Richard II*, and so he was creating the demand, and the supply always lagged behind him.

Mangan never knew the passages Brother Buster Clare wanted memorized. 'History was never meant to be *à-la-Clare*,' Mangan had said to me grandly at the start of the year.

'Why don't you learn it anyway?' I asked him. 'It only takes a few minutes.'

Mangan pursed his broad and yet delicate lips. 'I won't enter into a conspiracy with Buster to belittle Napoleon with memorized lines and such.'

Mangan would therefore spend nearly the entire year standing on the rostrum within reach of Buster for easy cuffing over the ears.

'*Mavourneen*, you are the most wilful, stubborn and immensely stupid student I have had in twenty years. Are you too good for Robert's *Modern History*? You say you are, *mavourneen*? What did you say? Did you say *you are*?'

I used to see a composure, a serenity, and contentment of a kind on Mangan's face as Buster Clare boxed his ears, still calling him *mavourneen*, that ironic Celtic endearment.

Mangan had always been like this. I had seen him take beatings and humiliations because of some inscrutable point of honour. For refusing to take interest in a cricket match say, and languidly turning his back on the game. Or for just being late, of course. You could see in Mangan's rigid standards even when it came to being unpunctual the future monk who would sleep in his own coffin as a *memento mori*, and rise at three-thirty to sing Matins, before going out into frosty fields to milk or feed the beasts. Mangan was deliberately saving up all his punctuality for his grand monastic career, for a routine worth being routine about.

In the meantime his lateness was legendary in Edgar Street. The year before, when our class had been in the Physics room, sitting at the long experiment benches under the tutelage of Brother Basher Bryant, there had occurred what I thought of as the crowning instance of Mangan's unworldly lateness for plain events.

Brother Bryant was choirmaster and fourth-year Physics teacher, and was not really so much more ferocious than anyone else despite his nickname. But he had put Mangan on a warning not to be late again. At nine-thirty one morning, the warned Mangan, heroically late, crept in the back door. Basher had his back to us and was writing some Physics formula on the blackboard. Mangan stood blushing, ready to surrender. But when Basher kept talking over his shoulder and did not turn, Mangan dropped to his knees, knee-walked in under the Physics bench with his school bag, and sheltered there. Those who saw this whispered, 'Typical bloody

Mangan.' Dahdah, who was then still at St Pat's and
Matt's familiar, filled Matt in on what had happened,
and I saw Matt begin to laugh, turning a vivid,
preternatural, tell-tale pink, as he always did when
trying to suppress hilarity. Dahdah had, of course,
whispering rights which were far more broad than those
of my fellow pupils, but if he used them recklessly, Matt
– who dwelt where pink was merely a notion – would
unwittingly give him away like this.

It has to be said that all those Australian adolescents,
though they thought Mangan a dingbat, kept the
convict code. Mangan could have sat there all day,
his textbook out on his knees, unreported, invisibly
following the lesson and noting down Basher's homework
requirements; if Basher had not come perambulating
around the back of the room orating as he went.
Thus he found Mangan, as fully employed as any
student could be, but as so often wrongly and even
grotesquely located. Mangan was ordered out. When
Basher asked Mangan what he had been doing there,
and whether he thought it was comic, Mangan said,
'I was hiding out of embarrassment.' This seemed
to make Basher angrier, but I know Mangan was
speaking the truth. He took six from the strap, the
quintessential Christian Brother weapon, a number of
strips of leather sewn together but with – according to
an unreliable legend amongst school boys – a hacksaw
blade included between the middle layers.

Mythologizing about the strap occupied a great part
of the time of younger Christian Brother boys. Some
Brothers were rumoured to practise giving it in the
secrecy of their cells. Some – we believed – stiffened
the thing, others made it more flexible. (We were not,
of course, aware of any Freudian imagery in our legend-
making.) The Brothers had frequently enough told us that
we boys and their own community were the totality of

their world. We imagined, therefore, that they spent all their free time thinking of us, whether it be in terms of charity or of punishment.

Yet it was through Basher Bryant that I had got a glimpse the year before of the fact that these men were indeed like others, and that like others they sought an existence of their own, that devotion to us was not their complete definition, and that the communal and institutional were not enough.

Our group would sometimes take to the streets on Sunday. We did not want to break things or to ambush anyone. But ennui made us restive. We were looking for something Homebush and Strathfield were hiding from us, daring the sky to deliver the unexpected. Dahdah, who was already talking restively of being a seminarian, Mangan, Larkin and myself argued over the existence of God, for which there were some very nifty proofs in Sheahan's *Apologetics*, a text we'd studied the year before. We would collect Matt Tierney on our way.

We walked expatiating amongst the suburban bungalows. Mangan knew the *Hound of Heaven* by heart, and as we passed the low brick fences, would recite it as if it too were a proof.

'I fled him down the labyrinthine ways of my own heart.'

Even, and perhaps particularly in the rain were we likely to go walking. Mrs Tierney released Matt to our care as long as he wore his thin grey raincoat. But I had escaped the house without coat or hat. This was on the one-in-a-hundred chance that girls were encountered. The one-in-a-thousand that Curran somehow was out and about that afternoon. Curran would say, 'He's so distracted by sublime thought he doesn't know it's raining.' Yet even I knew Curran was so stable she had that sense most of the young don't – the sense to come in out of the rain.

We would reach the school and sit for a while by the oval, looking at its vacant sabbath green. And then we would find ourselves moving amongst the buildings. Hoping for a glimpse of a Brother, of their lives without us. As we went we might recite *Hamlet* off by heart – it was our Shakespeare play for that year, and Brother Moose Davitt, who came from the same educational school as Buster, considered it safest if we learned every word by heart and Verity's notes on the text as well.

We had come to the Physics room that afternoon, and the door was mysteriously open. Our own room, open on a Sunday! In a society without theft we did not expect the worst, but there was no way we wouldn't look in.

Basher Bryant was there, at the top demonstration bench. He stood reflectively, a glass of whisky before him and a bottle by the sink. He saw us, put the glass at once in the sink, and came rushing towards us. He was brittly welcoming. 'Hello, boys, how are you today?' And we were anxiously smiling to explain ourselves away. 'We're just passing and saw the open door.'

'Do you often come up here on Sundays?' he asked, as if he wasn't entirely pleased that we did.

'Hard to keep away from the place, Bra.'

That was the common form of address. '*Bra*' for 'Brother'. Another instance of the Australian passion for shortening words.

But it was astounding what we had seen. Basher taking a private drink. Why did he need it? He had the company of the other Brothers. They occupied their hill in utter amity, a happy band. The comradeship was astounding, we were told by the Brother who came around to convince us to join. Why did Br Bryant need to drink solitary, severe liquor?

Now I know what warnings I should have taken from the sight, and how he must have genially cursed us. Would we mention it to someone? he must have wondered. The principal, Brother Callan? Our parents? Of course, he did not recognize how odd we were, and how long we'd keep his banal, innocent little secret.

The Brother who came around the classes now to urge us to consider succeeding Basher, Moose, Buster or Dinny in the Order's ranks, had that task as a full-time job.

'Ask yourself if God may not be sending you a signal. Look at the men who teach and guide you. Are you man enough to bear with them the vows of poverty, chastity and obedience. Remember this, the denial of a vocation will lead to the loss of your immortal soul. How many laymen out there plagued by drink and unhappiness, would have found salvation within the Brotherhood?'

I tried to imagine whether my father, moving like someone laden with questions amongst the tomato stakes at the bottom of the yard at 7 Loftus Crescent, might have somehow been meant to be Brother Keneally?

'I've known plenty of boys who have entered the Juniorate without knowing for certain whether they have a vocation, but in the spirit that it was better to find out than to lose one's immortal soul. Those who find they are not then called are able to leave with honour and without reproach and with a clear sense of what God's will is for them, and so to enter the holy state of matrimony without self-doubt.'

Whenever Brothers mentioned *the holy state of matrimony*, I thought for some reason of a dark-complexioned girl in a blue dress. Not Bernadette Curran, strangely. I didn't think of children nor did I think directly of sex. One perverse part of the daydream, sadly or not, was of how that essential girl would look when you told her, 'I have a vocation.' What drama in dull Strathfield. 'I have to renounce you, for the sake of both our salvations.'

I did not read the pallor and the normal lines of stress and neurosis in the faces of brothers and priests, though I was aware they were there and wondered why. I saw only myself with my Fix-a-Flexed hair in a week of no pimples renouncing the girl in the virgin blue dress, and we were both incandescent and as lovely and unearthly as a tapestry.

I always knew I wouldn't be a Brother though. I didn't want to do the walk-away from the girl in the blue dress just to spend the rest of my life correcting kids' homework and acting outraged because they hadn't finished some essay. I looked to the bigger fights involving the priesthood – St Francis and nature, St Vincent and poverty, Pius XII and Communism. Sometimes in fantasy I was a monk of total silence, like Mangan would be. Sometimes I was a vocal pastor. Just once the girl in the blue dress saw me from a distance and was awed by something broader than our mutual splendour.

But all that was a fantasy. I didn't want to be a priest. I wanted to be a composer, a writer, an orator and possibly all three. But again, an occasional clerical fantasy. I was a priest, and women turned their eyes to me, sad for what I was and could not be for them.

What I was certain about was that I did not want to be a Christian Brother. You didn't get canonized, you didn't become a bishop, and as far as I knew, you didn't get your thoughts or your poetry widely published.

A priest named Father Byrne did the bigtime recruiting, the recruiting for the seminary of the archdiocese of Sydney, from which ordained priests, not humble Brothers, emerged. The minor seminary was located at Springwood in the Blue Mountains, and was the institution into which Dahdah had recently vanished.

Father Byrne the persuader was thin and ageless, though certainly not more than forty years. He was very pale but not with the paleness of disappointment. More the paleness of having prayed at night. He was not one of the surfing, tennis-playing, golfing curates Australians seemed to like for their human touch. There was something too challenging about him for that. He had come down from the mountain top where there weren't any tennis courts, where scalding divine light hid every detail of the landscape.

Even now I think he was wonder-struck with the doctrine of Transubstantiation, with what others mocked, the transformation of the substance of the bread and wine into the body and blood of Christ by the word of the priest.

'This religion that makes cannibals of its members,' *The Rock* would thunder. 'They actually believe they eat the flesh and drink the blood!'

But we all had niftier minds than that. We ate the *appearances* of bread, the *appearances* of wine. How could outsiders fail to understand that? Malice was, of course, the answer.

'By your word,' Father Byrne would say to us. 'By the word of an ordinary man. But are you an ordinary man? You've been transformed by ordination. You have given up the joy of the earthly generation of Christians so that Christ may make use of your words and thereby enter Christians under the guise of homely elements like bread and wine.'

It was generally early in the year, when the humidity was strong and the blowflies were active, and before our plans for university were too settled, that the priests came to raise this other possibility. Some of them, a little more worldly than Father Byrne, appealed to ambition.

'Imagine the pride of this school, its Brothers and students on the day you are ordained to the priesthood in St Mary's Cathedral or even – in special cases – in St Peter's Basilica in Rome. Imagine then the joy of this school and of your parents if you should be consecrated a Bishop. Imagine then further what it would be for St Pat's if one of its sons was elevated to the College of Cardinals. For His Eminence Cardinal Gilroy attended an ordinary Brothers school and was an ordinary boy like you.'

We had seen Cardinal Gilroy distantly, proceeding in his scarlet cap and facings and accompanied by auxiliary bishops and monsignors in purple, and by clergy of lesser plumage, at the opening of new churches and new schools. It was the truth! He was native born. He had a slightly beaky but identifiably Irish face which you might have found on a parent, but he had gravity as well, and he would vent his resident Australian voice in a pulpit orator's delivery, which elevated its tones far above the utterance of ordinary people. Since his nomination as a Cardinal a year or two past, the newspapers ran occasional pieces about the likelihood of his being the next Pope.

Again, a daydream! ABC Radio returning to ask aged Brothers and grownup former students what they remembered of the new Pope. What sort of boy was he? Asking the girl in the blue dress, who in her grief had scarcely aged, but was fixed in her blue adolescent loss. Asking Bernadette Curran and the Frawley girls. 'There *was* something about him,' Bernadette Curran would say. I saw her in this fantasy as barely aged too and wearing still her maroon Santa Sabina uniform.

After the priest had gone again, non-Celestials of the kind who hung on the Paragon milk bar in the Boulevarde in Strathfield, who sang the latest pop songs and had never heard of Mahler or GMH – fellows that is like genial Freddie Ford – would come up to Matt and pretend the priesthood was an option for him and say, 'Gunna break all the sheilas' hearts, Mattie?'

And Matt would frame the answer with his handsome white lips. 'Aw, don't think they'd want me, Freddie. I think I'd bring down the tone in the seminary.'

Freddie Ford was the sort of boy who went to the Stockade, the big combined toilets and changing rooms, at lunchtime with his mates. They would stand in turns in front of the one mirror and work frankly on their hair, slicking it lovingly back, as if it wasn't theirs but someone else's, as if they were barbers enjoying their work. Freddie was a boy of a different kind of honour and daydream, a boy kindly, mocking, sensual, deliberately neither a prefect nor a scholar, and happy with his age and surroundings. Mangan called Freddie and the others *narcissists*. But you couldn't call any of this public lunchtime hairdressing narcissistic, because they did it in front of their mates, communally, trying to look like Farley Granger or Montgomery Clift. Slyly and secretly at home, I tried to make mine look like Chatterton's, Viney managed to make his look like Beethoven's, and on top of that we felt morally superior. For we worked in guilty and exhaustive secrecy and wouldn't have confessed under torture to caring about these things.

At the start of the year, when Father Byrne came around to canvass us, the idea of the priesthood for me seemed preposterous. University would be the good thing. I would join the Newman Society and talk about scholastic philosophy, and perhaps Curran or the recurrent girl in blue would be there. Despite the splendour of the vestments and sacraments, I couldn't see much sense in being a plumply irascible, suburban priest like Monsignor Loane of St Martha's of Strathfield – Pop Loane the school kids called him – who played golf on Mondays and worried a lot about the Silver Circle, the numbers-like betting game on which St Martha's depended for a lot of its income. You wouldn't have ever heard Father Hopkins S.J. mention any Silver Circle! Father Byrne himself was quite a suitable model, but a threatening one, in that there seemed no flamboyance in his nature, no room for Hopkinsian poetry or broad gesture.

But although I didn't want to be a priest as far as I knew, and did not wish to occupy some Curran-less pulpit from which the Silver Circle results fell, I still queued up in the corridor with other people who wondered if they might be called. It was according to Father Byrne's advice, and all the advice I had heard since childhood, better to err on the side that you might be *called*, as the phrase went, and it got you out of Buster Clare's General Maths anyhow. And I was also within the guidelines: 'Do you go to Mass more than once a week? Do you find yourself engaged in spiritual debates when some of your mates are more concerned about the things of the world? Do you spend most of your life in a state of Sanctifying Grace through regular Acts of Contrition and regular attendances at the confessional? Etc, etc.' All that applied to me.

'I don't think my sense of vocation has crystallized yet,' I told Father Byrne when my turn to talk to him came.

That was a good verb, I knew. Brother Dinny McGahan would have liked that word.

'Then be calm and pray to our Blessed Mother,' said Father Byrne. 'The Mother of all of us. I don't know what would have happened to me without Her.'

We would all later find out that he was telling the truth about this. While he spoke, he looked to the ledge in the corner of the room on which the Madonna stood in blue and white robes. The Virgin Mother Saint Bernadette had seen at Lourdes. Even though I now know, in the smart-alec way all we former Brothers' boys now know, that Mary would not have been blue and white, would not have had Saxon or Celtic features, but would have been a small, brown and glittering-eyed, Bedouin-like woman, I did not doubt the force of what Father Byrne was saying then and I do not doubt it now. He was talking about an utterly literal kinship. He was talking about his Dreaming, if you like. The balance of his world depended on it. You looked into his pale face and did feel the appeal and temptation to be a young priest, rosary in hand, in a cold church after all the people had left, keeping the Virgin's real company at the altar rails.

'I suppose if I'm not sure at the end of the year,' I told him blithely, covering my bets, 'I could go to the seminary maybe after a year at uni.'

I wanted those poets and novelists, and the chance to argue with secular philosophers and to wrongfoot humanist professors with my Thomism.

'I must counsel you very seriously,' said Father Byrne, leaning forward, 'that is not the best way. There is a spirit of secularism and disbelief at the university. I know many a young man who followed that line: first my degree and then the priesthood. By the time they'd finished their degree, under the influence of atheistic philosophers from Marx to Nietzsche to Bertrand Russell, they'd lost their faith. The seminary is in any case a complete education – English, European Languages, History. But as well as that, of course, Philosophy, and Moral and Dogmatic Theology and Canon Law.'

'Would I be allowed to try to write poetry or novels?' I wanted to know.

The novelist priest. A sort of G. K. Chesterton with a collar. Monsignor Ronald Knox wrote murder mysteries.

'Subject to proper authority,' said Father Byrne. 'I had a seminary friend who wrote poetry on a regular basis and had it published in the *Messenger of the Sacred Heart*.'

There was some confusion for me in this news of his friend's literary glories. I'd read the *Messenger of the Sacred Heart*, and a lot of its verse was obvious, rhyme-y stuff, full of clichés (ugh!) and none of the verbal and theological thunder of GMH.

'I'll be back in May,' said Father Byrne, 'and we may be able to speak then.'

Mangan didn't go to see Father Byrne. Mangan was beyond all that reassurance and urging stuff. He was shooting straight for the stars. He didn't want anyone trying to persuade him to go to the Sydney Diocesan Seminary. Rather than chat with Father Byrne, he would remain in class, doing penance within cuffing reach of Brother English.

Father Byrne was in any case not the only messenger from the spiritual world. There was still the free orchestral concert every Sunday afternoon in Sydney's massive, nineteenth-century Town Hall.

Sometimes the conductor was Sir Eugene Goossens, a bald, smooth-looking man. Quite famous, in a few years time he would be found with what Australian Customs said were pornographic items in his luggage and would be primly exiled for it. The awful thing was that some Australians would be oddly comforted that he was so found out. It just showed you! Artistic types.

An Oxbridge aesthete could not have folded himself more interestingly into his seat than Mangan did, or laid a finger more ponderingly over his lips, or become more lost. I wanted to be able to do that, but my bones weren't long enough. During the entire recital, Mangan would not once open his eyes. He was away on the plateau where Tchaikovsky, Bach and Debussy held discourse. The Frawley girls and Curran, with their nose for pretension, would nudge each other and point to him.

Afterwards we would descend to the train, and walk each other miles home from wherever we disembarked. One night we all walked Curran to her home on the hill behind St Pat's. The Currans lived in a standard brick cottage which was nonetheless rendered special by the cleverness and good looks of the Curran girls, Bernadette and her two younger sisters. Mr Curran, who worked for the State government, was as good-looking as a father in a film – a little like Fred MacMurray as a matter of fact. And there were plenty of older actresses that weren't as impressive as Mrs Curran. The same could have been said for my mother, on whose looks everyone commented, though for some reason that caused me to squirm.

As Mrs Curran gave us tea, I said to her, 'I don't know about becoming a priest. Mrs Curran, I wonder if all your beautiful daughters would wait till I find out.'

Everyone laughed, Rose Frawley indulgently. 'What a drongo,' she said softly to her tea.

Mrs Curran said, 'I think you'd better stay at home with us, Mick.'

I felt secure, and knew I was staying home at least until recognized by the world. But just in case, what I'd said would make a good story for her to tell the ABC should I win the Nobel Prize at twenty-three or become Pope.

III

The upstairs flat in Loftus Crescent, which we had rented
since the Second World Cataclysm, sat above a down-
stairs which had been rented for a similar length of time
to a family called the Bankses. I did not realize it, since
I took him for granted, that my father had startling
ways of describing people. He was, in fact, a wordsmith
comparable in his way to Gerard Manley Hopkins, a sort
of bush poet who got not enough honour for it from his
son.

Instead of describing the unutterable – 'Thou mastering me, God!' – he described the Bankses. It would
often be at night, while, say, wakeful in bed, I read
Silas Marner as my parents listened to some despicable
big band, far beneath the attention of a Mahler-fancier,
on the radio in the living room. I would overhear my
mother mention the Bankses, the struggle she had with
Mrs Banks over the use of the one laundry and the
clothesline, and then get my father's response. It was
easy to overhear conversations in our small flat and
had been since I was a child. The two small bedrooms,
narrow kitchenette, kitchen-dining room, living room
and bathroom were jammed close together.

Mr Banks was a hefty man, a railway guard, whom my
father called a 'flobble-gutted, wombat-headed garper',
an onomatopoeic combination whose inventiveness, if
not its unkindness, GMH might well have approved
of.

I heard my father describe little red-haired Mrs Banks –
with the robust political incorrectness of his day – as 'silly as

a gin at a christening'. Lanky Verna Banks, their daughter, was, 'straight up and down like a yard of pump water'.

My mother said he got his imagery, his bush word-smithery, from his Irish mother, who had had a range of earthy things to say about the people who'd surrounded her in the valley of the Macleay earlier in the century. The coming of in-house plumbing therefore hadn't yet cancelled her image about pump water in her son's mouth, and it ran forth and hit Verna Banks behind the ear in Homebush in 1952.

Poor Verna. I carried in childhood like a writ against her the memory that late in the war, when the Bankses put on their daughter's twenty-first birthday party and somehow got a keg of beer into Flemington Town Hall for the party, they'd had to invite boys from the nearby air force depot to make up the crowd. Verna danced with a tall, leering Leading Aircraftsman while the band played *Coming in on a Wing and a Prayer*. I did not have the imagination to see Verna as a victim, stuck with Mrs Banks. What must it have been like for a daughter with dreams to listen to her mother's horrifying misnomers and malapropisms? I had myself heard Mrs Banks call camouflage *flamagage,* the actress Maureen O'Hara *Moran Harara*, M&B tablets *ham and beef tablets*, pneumonia *pew-mania*.

The Bankses had turned out to be readers of *The Rock*. Mrs Banks in particular quoted everything that was in it. 'I've never had anything against you Romanian Catholics,' she had been telling my mother every week since we moved down from the bush ten years past.

One night, I overheard my mother say with some venom, 'Mrs Banks came to me today and asked whether I was worried about Michael and John. I asked her why, and she said that there were so many stories in *The Rock* of brothers interfering with boys, that some of them had to be true.'

'This comes from Evatt,' my father said. 'Beating the sectarian drum. Evatt is the choir master, and old Banksie is the monkey's arse.'

But my mother's concerns were more local. 'Even if there was occasionally something like that, I think the boys would tell me.'

'Chrysler Six!' said my father. 'You're not taking Mrs Banks as a guide to the real bloody world, are you?'

Yes, I would have liked to say. Dinny is interfering with me. He has given me Graham Greene to read, and W. H. Auden, and he's played some Mahler and pointed out GMH's *Thou mastering me God!* And I will never be the same.

For I was not only reading *Silas Marner*, I was reading *Brighton Rock*, in which the young English razor gangster felt a Manichean disgust for the flesh of his girlfriend. This wasn't just a story about gangster fighting gangster. This was about salvation and flesh and spirit. It was like finding out that James Cagney was really a walking battleground between angels of spirit and flesh. Who gave a damn about Mrs Banks and *The Rock*?

The crass accusers of *The Rock* knew nothing either about the humane face of Brother Digger Crichton, simple and generous soul, veteran of World War I, who had seen the world's deadly pomps and now taught nothing but woodwork. He was a natty little man whose cassock showed the marks neither of glue nor nails nor sawdust.

He had unwittingly developed one quasi-sporting and religious rite of his own. The Rugby League goalposts were kept in his huge woodwork room throughout summer, and towards the end of the first term every year, about Easter time, they would be carried to the oval by crews of junior woodworkers, one pole at a time, along with the cross bar, striped in the middle – where all the most perfect goals sailed over – with the school's black and blue and gold. A seasonal rite for which he chose only the finest boy carpenters! Two years before I had somehow cack-handedly assembled a glass-fronted bookcase which my mother keeps to this day crammed with the textbooks of our childhood. I was not sufficiently accomplished at tenon joints ever to take part in that sacrament of the posts.

Though we Leaving Certificate boys no longer took woodwork, occasionally Digger Crichton came to us to give Religion class when Dinny or Buster was ill. What he told us about on such occasions was always the Red Baron, and the controversy over who had shot him down, the Canadians as the history books incorrectly said, or the Australians.

At sixteen, I could still see in Brother Crichton's tale a collision of the old world and the new, something about which as it turned out I would later try to write a number of novels. But of fascination to me too was the fact that somehow the Western Front had not made Digger Crichton worldly. It was as if it had been so horrible that he understood that should he become knowing and ironic, he would lose himself in a morass of cynicism. And so he remained an innocent. Always with a childlike open face. He never gave anyone the strap either. The strap was simply not part of his repertoire.

He had come to Strathfield in 1928 with the first Brothers, and had been here ever since and was happy at how it had gone. More than a thousand boys! More than a battalion. In fact, some battalions, he told us, got down to about a hundred and fifty men towards the end of the war. So we were his super battalion upon which no artillery would fire.

Listening then to Digger Crichton telling us about the death of Von Richthofen, the Red Baron! Would that young German aristocrat ever have believed that his name would come up so often in Religion classes in the antipodes?

Brother Crich or Digger Crichton was a dispatch rider in the Third Australian Division, and his mount was a former Queensland racehorse. On a spring day in 1918, he was riding his horse eastwards up the road to Vaux-sur-Somme carrying a message to the headquarters of the 52nd Australian Battalion. The Australians had managed to stop the great German spring offensive here, astride the Somme, that great river of blood.

We can all envisage – from repeated descriptions – the road down which Brother Crichton delivers his message. It is a little sunken, and on the rise to his left a number of Australian batteries are in place, and Lewis gunners with their guns set on a swivel and equipped with anti-aircraft sights. Dispatch rider Crichton and his horse are alarmed when a big Sopwith Camel aircraft appears, filling the sky, low enough to clip his horse's ears. The horse thinks so too and skews sideways. The huge red nose of the Sopwith fills Trooper Crichton's vision, but then is gone and succeeded instantly, a few inches higher still, by the enormous all red machine of the Baron. The Baron has the British Sopwith in his sights and is hammering away at it.

'The Sopwith, boys, was flown by one Lieutenant May of the Royal Flying Corps.'

That's why we liked Brother Crichton. In his Religion classes Lieutenant May had equal weight with Saint Therese of Lisieux and Saint Anthony of Padua.

The Lewis gunners along the road and on the ridge beside Trooper Crichton began firing as soon as the British Sopwith was past.

'Now, boys, a mile to the south over the church

steeple of Corbie I could see another Sopwith, and this was flown as it turned out by a Canadian pilot, Lieutenant Brown. Brown would later be given all the credit for shooting down Baron Von Richthofen. The books say that earlier, before he peeled away, Brown had fired some shots at the Baron, but that was just before I turned up. I must tell you that I think Lieutenant Brown is sincere in believing he caused fatal damage to the Red Baron, he later wrote a book about it. Well . . . I think most men could tell a brief lie, but not then write an entire book on it.

'At the time I saw the Red Baron he was hugging the terrain, flying very well and right on Lieutenant May's hammer. He was in full control and expecting another victory. The glory and vanity of the world were however about to desert him. Because it was when he crossed the ridge, following Lieutenant May, that I saw one of the Australian Lewis gunners open up and get him. The doctors agree with what I saw. They later found that he'd been shot from below and through the heart. Lieutenant Brown claimed to have shot him from above. There's an inconsistency, you see.

'After the Lewis gunners got him, the Baron swerved back eastward towards Jerry's lines. But now you could tell he was out of control, and he crashed on the furthest edge of the ridge the artillery stood on. This ridge was open to enemy fire, but soldiers rushed from everywhere to see if he could be saved. I galloped over there myself. The Germans, for a time believing Brown's version which was published in all the papers, said he was alive when he crashed and one of us shot him. But no Australian has that on his soul, boys. We would have lifted him out and shaken him by the hand. Look in the official war history -- the Red Baron is already dead, and is buried with full honours by Australian men in slouch hats.'

And Crich is right. There is such a remarkable picture. Lanky Aussies firing into the air over the Baron, whom everyone admired. Boys from the bush in a fusillade over a prince from Prussia.

'Join me now, boys, in praying for the soul of Baron Von Richthofen and all the faithful departed.'

It didn't strike us as odd to say an Our Father and three Hail Marys for a thirty-five-year-dead Baron. Some of us had prayed for other historical figures. Mangan had once attended Mass for the repose of the soul of Byron. I sometimes – while reciting the rosary – remembered Talleyrand, who'd been a bishop before he had been a statesman and had a lot to expiate. Through the Communion of Saints, we were connected from Strathfield and Homebush to history's giant shifts and huger sinners.

Brother Crichton's story had potency for me even after I became a Celestial. For all of us. It was a classic version of the great brought down by the humble. The humble then being denied the credit, since that was the way of the world. Even now that I had read *Sweeney Agonistes*, Trooper Crichton's fable still fascinated me.

Dinny was remarkable because he would appear at the elbow of this boy or that and present them with some special task they had not thought of themselves, a task which related them to the larger universe. In that spirit he came to me one autumn morning and said, 'Young Keneally, ah . . . ah . . . I want you to enter the Newmans Society Essay Prize and win something for the school. I suggest that since you're so crazy about Gerard Manley Hopkins, you should write about him.' He had a slim grey book in his hands. 'Here is a *Kenyon Critics* essay on Gerard Manley Hopkins, and otherwise with your

record last year and this, I think you would be a good
. . . ah . . . bet.'

Essay prizes were the first blaze writers made on
their trail to greatness. Didn't they say on the back
cover of Evelyn Waugh novels, 'Evelyn Waugh won the
Hughenden Essay Prize at Oxford.' The upshot was, of
course, in every case an endless flow of grand fiction. I
could see already before my eyes the red back covers of
my Penguins. 'Keneally won the Newman Essay Prize . . .'

Yet my reputation for English was perhaps an inflated
one in Dinny's eyes. It was based on the fact that
the year before I'd come first in the state for Christian Brothers Schools. This sounded promising. But it
was slightly suspect in reality.

That year big Brother Moose Davitt had taught us
English. His method was to sit at the chemistry bench at
the front of the room with his leather case opened before
him. Inside it were limp-covered pulp Westerns which
were his preferred reading. And a supply of tobacco
and cigarette papers out of which, as he expatiated on
Shakespeare, he rolled masses of skinny cigarettes for
consumption out of class hours. He was frumpy, Moose.
His soutane was carelessly kept and sprinkled with ash,
he had large bullish features, and he was dearly loved by
all of us. As his hands worked in the opened leather case,
he advised us that he was slow to anger, but to be wary
when it came, and that the only thing he couldn't really
stand was a boy horse-laughing.

'If you're wise boys, you won't horse laugh. It drives
me mad, and I can't help it.'

Moose's method of preparing us for exams was rather
like Buster Clare's method of teaching History. Faced
with a large poem like Keats' *Hyperion*, he would say,
'I don't know about this one. It was on the paper four
years ago. I might go and test out Dinny about it over
the weekend.'

For Dinny McGahan was stellar enough to have been given the job of setting the examination for all the Christian Brothers Schools. Moose had a special talent for enraging Dinny, for teasing probabilities out of him. For gauging exam paper omens in what was said over the flummery at the monastic table in the Brothers' house on the corner of Edgar Street.

The next Monday Moose would be back with his brief-case of Verity's Shakespeare, Romantic poetry, cowboy novelettes and tobacco.

'I think we'd better do *Hyperion*, boys. I said to Dinny at dinner on the weekend, I don't think I'll bother teaching the boys that. And he said, Ah . . . ah . . . I tell you, your boys better be prepared with *Hyperion* if they want to do well.'

Thus the odds on *Hyperion* had shortened, and Moose explained to us what the poem was all about, and then set us to learn it and its notes and its study guide all by heart. Everything had equal value with Moose – the merest footnote by some junior English academic, and the highest imagery of John Keats. In fact, footnotes were probably more useful for exam purposes, for they explained the Classical allusions.

. . . she would have ta'en
Achilles by the hair and bent his neck;
Or with a finger stay'd Ixion's wheel.
Her face was large as that of Memphian sphinx . . .

This material represented in many ways the world Mangan and I would have preferred to Homebush. Other boys said, 'What's it got to do with getting a job, Brother?' Mangan and I really kindled to Wordsworth's *On Westminster Bridge* and Keats' *On First Looking into Chapman's Homer*. We thought these men were reporting a real world, and didn't understand that they were lost souls, too, in the moils of a squalid Industrial Revolution and trying to ignore it.

We had both already written poetry like theirs. Some of it still exists, composed all over the flyleaves of textbooks. With its mixture of Romanticism and theology, it is as embarrassing as teenage love letters. It is in fact a series of love letters, since I saw it as near publishable and likely to impress Curran with its promise when published amongst my *Early Poems*. None of it will be brought into play in these pages.

But back to the 1951 exam. On top of baiting Dinny, by the end of the year, through methods which included exploiting his spies in the senior year who showed him the sort of questions Dinny was setting in term exams there, Moose had a sophisticated betting sheet, and we followed it. In English exam terms, we were the equivalent of the first steroid takers in the decathlon. As an unnatural advantage, we knew as no other Christian Brothers' boys did which areas to concentrate on. The result was that I was first in the state, my name published in the *Catholic Weekly* to the gratification of my parents. And my repute with Dinny McGahan was set somewhat higher than I knew I quite deserved.

Dinny probably had a more accurate sense of my attributes as an athlete than as an English scholar. During a meeting of the athletics team, all ages, he said, 'Ah . . . stand up young Keneally. Now you see, boys, you don't have to be a champion like Peter McInnes to make a contribution. There's a boy who'll never be a champion but who has a fine time running and training and can get placed in inter-school events for us and even occasionally win one.'

The smaller boys looked at me. An average hero. I didn't feel offended at all. There was something that suited the Australian self-image in such a definition. I was a battler. If all the conditions were right, my chance of a 220 or 440 yards victory had been pronounced on by Dinny.

'Black, black, rickety rack,' the younger members of the athletics team would chant in the event of a chance win,

> SPC is on the track,
> Blue black, blue black gold . . .

Dinny did understand now that I was so good on GMH because I was neglecting the broader sweep of writers. Curran was doing Honours English too, and when I talked to her on the train to and from concerts, it was obvious to me that she was covering the field. 'Have you done much on the Gothic novel yet?' she asked me. It was clear she had, under the tutelage of some analytical Dominican nun. She was also covering the main eras of English poetry, and reading a few representatives in each case. The same with the novel. Whereas I tended to get fixated. I wasn't covering the whole pelagic expanse of literature. I was diving deeply enough to get the bends in a few places.

To console myself, I wrote on the flyleaf of my copy of GMH, *Michael K., Professor of Hopkinsian Idiosyncrasy*.

I made sure I knew all I could find out about Hopkins' 'sprung rhythm', and when I found myself reciting it according to what the Kenyon critics said it should sound like, I discovered that the only way to read Hopkins' poetry was in a sort of incantatory voice, in an intonation a little sub- or supra-human.

> Earnest, earthless, equal, attuneable, vaulty,
> voluminous, . . . stupendous
> Evening strains to be time's vast, womb-of-all,
> home-of-all, hearse-of-all night.

Once Dinny McGahan played us a record of Dylan Thomas reading his *Poem in October*, and Dylan Thomas seemed to know all that, even though he was an alcoholic about to die. Welsh intonation, which I'd never heard before in my life. That – I told myself – was the intonation for reading Hopkins. A bardic intonation.

I already knew that novelty gave you a chance in literary contests. I would put up this incantation theory in my essay, padded out with a lot of plagiarized critical jargon. And beyond it all, I would strain to utter the grandeur of what Hopkins was trying to do.

> With: Our evening is over us; our night whelms,
>   whelms, and will end us.
> Only the beak-leaved boughs dragonish damask
>   the tool-smooth bleak light . . .

Curran though seemed to think Hopkins was just another interesting poet in the Honours English course. I dreamed I would read something of him to her one day, and she would be transformed.

IV

In line with being a Celestial, I did not seem to myself
to have changed much physically since the week or so
in the first year of high school when I first began to
understand Latin declensions, and simultaneously, in
a flash, like falling in love, understand Pythagoras's
Theorem after a long stand-off with it. That first year
of high school was the year when from being an infant
sleepwalker I first became a serious academic contender
and got to like the feeling of moderate scholarly success.
Now, in my sixteenth year I was a far more turbulent
spirit, and felt that something massive was about to
descend upon me, but I saw the turmoil not as sexual
but as utterly spiritual and aesthetic. I was not aware
of any increase in erections, which I was still and for
whatever reason too innocent to take for what they
were. I was not aware of the surge of testosterone.
I may have been a late developer, and uttering that
idea is not offensive to me. But really I don't think
so. I think I was what people talk about when they
mention the monastic temperament and sex: a case of
sublimation. A case of culture defeating nature.

In the Easter Week retreat senior boys went through
– three James Joycean days of silence and sessions from
a retreat master, generally a Passionist or Redemptorist
priest -- the retreat master had told us with a false matter-
of-factness that there might be some mornings when we
woke up to find a stickiness on our upper legs.

This was said in the sermon on purity, and the sure road to damnation which *impurity* provided. The reference to stickiness caused Freddie and others to nudge each other, but I have to confess with some embarrassment I didn't know what he was talking about. Nor was I interested. It was like Honours Science – something I wasn't involved in.

Impure thoughts swam into the young mind, said the retreat master, as surely as brightly-coloured, poisonous fish frequented a reef. I knew at least that that was true. I remembered that a little earlier that year, I was for once walking on my own up Edgar Street, reading occasionally as I walked. It was Eliot's little book on what poetry was. Imagery, said Eliot. That was what it was. Everywhere, new and wonderful beasts of language falling from the sky! Imagery raining cats and dogs. That was the essence of poetry. Mind you, I also had a weakness for half-rhymes myself, and GMH wasn't against them and Wilfred Owen, the World War I soldier, had favoured them before the machine guns got him. But the image – that was everything. I could accept that proposition. No worries!

And in the midst of being enlightened by T. S. Eliot, a substantial image of a woman entered my head, a woman with bountiful breasts. And I knew that somewhere in her body was a place designed with her urgent consent to contain me. But where was it? I found that I didn't know and I wanted to. Not for any immediate purpose, though for an imminent purpose.

Who was that woman whose presence I sensed? Who was the girl in the blue dress? And how did they both relate to living women like the Frawley and Curran girls?

I cannot remember having suffered any guilt over this quandary. I don't think that I felt any need ever to confess it. But since I still remember it, it must have been a question of some force, since I paused on Strathfield's orderly pavement, a boy with a lurking pimple scar on his jawline and a manufactured hairstyle. A *faux* casual, that boy, who was one of the few in Strathfield to know that poetry was image, yet did not know how the race, the poets, the novelists, the Communion of Saints were generated.

Whatever all this meant, I didn't have the time to be a lascivious schoolboy. Instead, my demented energy was astounding to my parents and even myself. These days I would generally study till at least eleven o'clock at night, with 2BL the classical station on the radio in the lounge room, and me sprawled with a dozen books before it. Hence with the off-hand lack of thought of the adolescent, I now deprived my parents of the chance of chatting by the radio as it played more casual programmes.

This particular radio, which brought Handel and Mendelssohn to the young Homebush aesthete, was the very one my aunts Molly and Annie had bought to listen to the broadcast of the opening of the Harbour Bridge in 1932. Over it had come Test Matches, war news, the bells of peace brought on by atomic explosions in Japan, and speeches by Australian Prime Ministers. Through its mesh of valves came the death of Prime Minister Curtin, the accession of Ben Chifley, the election of Bob Menzies.

I would go to sleep after my parents, and wake about six o'clock ravenous for life and Eliot's promised images. Some mornings I went to Mass as Strathfield. I could have just as easily gone up to Flemington to Father Johnson's little church, but he was the sort of priest that rattled through the Latin, and I liked the greater solemnity of Father Byrne who now frequently said the early morning Mass at St Martha's. Maybe in outrageous vanity I hoped he would see me there and be moved to wonder. Had I made up my mind yet? Not for him to know how essential the olive-skinned beauty of Curran in her Santa Sabina uniform was to the systems of my world.

Then carrying the Globite bag every Australian boy carried to school in those years, I would walk joyfully towards Matt Tierney's, accomplishing my part-solitary, part-communal approach to school. On the way I might outline the scheme of my essay and draw down phrases from the high lake of imagery which seemed to be situated above my head. I would be at Matt's front door before eight, *sans* or *avec* Mangan, *sans* or *avec* having sighted Curran at the 414 bus stop or run into the Frawleys, and Mrs Tierney would take me through to the enclosed back verandah where Matt and I would sit together doing his Pass English – the sort of English they devised for kids who hadn't read Eliot's book and might spend the rest of their lives believing that poetry necessarily rhymed.

At that stage, of course, though it was a fairly well kept secret, there were superb Australian poets who knew what T. S. Eliot knew but who pursued what people call 'their own voices'. Judith Wright, a young woman who came from a grazing family from Armidale in Northern New South Wales, the area which was called New England. Kenneth Slessor, who was a journalist and editorial writer for Frank Packer at the *Daily Telegraph*. A. D. Hope, who taught English in Canberra; David Campbell, a farmer and former fighter pilot from the Canberra area. And then Douglas Stewart. The verse play was popular in the 1950s and Douglas Stewart had written two fine ones – *Fire on the Snow*, a play about Scott of Antarctica, and another on Ned Kelly the Australian hero-saint or brigand. These would soon, but too late for us, creep their way into the school curriculum and raise the supposition that perhaps poetry was possible in Australia. But on the mornings we did Pass English on Matt Tierney's back verandah, the idea which the examiners seemed to propose, and which I knew to be untrue, was that poetry had ended with Alfred Lord Tennyson.

Already I had been frenetically conscious for three hours as Matt and his mother conducted their normal contest over who had put his glasses where, which of his suit buttons should be done up and which left undone, and where his foldable white stick was.

After the full day's school work, Dinny – lean as a runner himself, nimble in movement and intent – already had our athletics team (the term *track team* was an Americanism which entered much later into Australian usage) training twice a week. Sometimes Matt would stay back with me, and we would practise running the bends with the Nugget Boot Polish tins, the Braille type rattling inside. Matt was game, thundering into a curve in the track, missing his direction, re-cueing his ear to the rattling type, and picking up speed again. In some such moments, I *was* simply liberated through fraternal love for the thwarted athlete in Matt, the child un-sighted in the womb by a chance infection.

Mangan would sometimes wait for us, his legs folded, his chin pensively held, a hermit in the grey serge suit of St Pat's. My similar coat, GMH still crushed into its vest pocket, and Matt's similar coat hung in the Stockade waiting for us to finish with our vulgar preoccupation with running the curve in the 220 yards.

Back with Matt to Shortland Avenue, then dawdle home with Mangan, calling at the Frawleys' on the way. Like a more accustomed adolescent in that: delaying going home if you could. On top of that, delicious hours of study lay ahead. In a life rich in experiences, I would later live as richly but never more so.

One such afternoon I was joking around with the Frawley girls, maybe introducing them to a bit of my execrable poetry, when Mr Frawley got back home from the Department of Railways.

Mr Frawley took me aside. 'Campbell's crowd attacked Saint Anthony's Home for Fallen Girls last night,' he told me. Saint Anthony's was a place where Catholic girls from the bush who got pregnant came to have their babies far from the severe stares of their bush townspeople.

'I think he gets some of his spies into the kitchens of these places,' said Mr Frawley. 'They work as cooks and dishwashers, and they talk to discontented girls who feel hard done by. And they tell them that Campbell will come and rescue them. These are girls that have just given birth to their children. He's not interested in the ones who are still pregnant. Some of Campbell's commandos got into the garden of Saint Anthony's last night and took away two girls. They thought they were going off to freedom in the city of their dreams. Silly young things!'

Saint Anthony's was in plain, suburban Ashbury, a place no more distinctive than Homebush. Mr Frawley's tale indicated that portentous dramas could occur even in Ashbury, tucked in as it was behind Ashfield, a mere stop on the Western Line.

'It's not going to happen again,' said Mr Frawley, whose whole tone was confidential anyhow, but who had become more confidential still. 'We have our agents too. This will be his only successful stop. But you watch how the next issue of *The Rock* will be full of these girls. He'll cast them as nuns. He'll cast their children as the illegitimate children of priests. You watch!'

After picking up such intelligence from Mr Frawley, who seemed to tell me things he didn't trouble others with, I would go home at last to a quick dinner, sometimes timing it for when my parents had finished their meal so that I would be left to read over the stew or the chops. Not because I abhorred the company of my parents so much as I loved reading in itself and because reading at the table was an accredited mark of brilliant young men. My mother would be able to say on some

ABC programme of the future, 'He always read at the table.'

Four blocks away, on the far side of the Western Line down which the electric trains rattled and the steam trains pulsed, Mangan listened to a relay from the BBC, the comedian Dick Bentley and *Much Binding in the Marsh*, and planned how to be heroically late for or ill-informed in some class the next day. From the BBC, he would come to school with mysterious English-isms like, 'I should cocoa.' (I don't know to this day how that cocoa or ko-ko is spelled.) He devoted his time to reading superfluous and obscure history and failing to learn Buster Clare's prescribed history. More biddable, I covered all those routine tasks as well, and went to bed late only after my mother had emerged once or twice from the front bedroom to urge me to do so. She could report *that* to the radio interviewer one day too.

Perhaps it was all the fuel that should have gone into overt sexual energy which made me burn over my studies at night, rise early again, walk all those miles, hold all those conversations and coruscate with all those yearnings.

The school dance may be one of the expected set pieces of memoirs of adolescence, but it was not an expected set piece for us. It was announced as a great social experiment – akin to universal male suffrage – and the news of it galvanized us in the early Strathfield winter. Who had dreamt up such a concept? Buster Clare? Mother Benignus? How had it got past their guard or seemed acceptable to them, this proposed and never-before-ventured-upon occasion both of grace and sin, involving St Pat's boys and the girls of Santa Sabina Dominican Convent.

It was unprecedented and un-recurrent, and we needed to be prepared. An elocution teacher named Miss Gibson, a robust woman with a throaty, smoker's voice and elegant vowels, came in and did her best in Brother Crichton's cleared woodwork room to teach us how to dance. Wiry-haired Peter O'Gallagher danced with Matt, since Peter had already been taught the steps. It was apparent that Matt wanted to take the learning of dance steps seriously, and in this too he showed an athletic elegance, though as in running he would pause now and then, his head cocked sideways, to listen to the sound of the nearby competitors' feet.

Mangan and I danced together, determined not to pick up this crass suburban skill. Could *La Belle Dame Sans Merci* do the two-step? Did Christina Rossetti bother with the foxtrot? Could it be imagined that GMH ever took a partner in the Pride of Erin? We despised the useful social skills we were being offered – after all, Mangan reasoned, Trappist monks didn't go to local hops. We went with deliberate clumsiness through Miss Gibson's motions. Our future would be innocent of dance floors.

Just the same, one dusk with the grateful beginning of chill to it, the hint of seasons of mist and mellow fruitfulness, I turned up at the Curran household. Mrs Curran always had me in if she had time, given that I was considered at least amusingly eccentric.

I told her I wanted to see if Bernadette would consent to be my partner at the dance. I imagined ideal conversations between us which certainly overrode the banal dance steps.

Mrs Curran went and got Bernadette from her room, where she was studying according to her eminently practical timetable. Entering the living room, Bernadette wore spotlessly all the items of the Santa Sabina uniform, and the shirt she had had on all day was still crisp and uncreased. Her shoes were off but her feet and legs were still encased in the brown hosiery the Santa Sabina girls wore. So astounding and perfect! In my chest I felt the possibility that we could drift away disembodied on clouds of Hopkinsian idiosyncrasy. She wore a wary yet indulgent smile, of the kind women always wear in the presence of madmen they are not utterly unfriendly towards. Wary because they knew the lunatic might make too much of their kindness.

'That would be good,' she said to my proposal. 'Dad's worried about who's going to walk home with me.'

This in mugger-less, murder-less Strathfield.

'We'll all walk home together,' I promised. 'Mangan, Matt, the Frawleys.' The Goodly Company. I could taste the eternal sweet mile and a quarter of that walk.

'I'll need to dance with other people too,' she said. 'That's the policy.' She laughed. 'I'd like to have a dance or two with someone who *can* dance.'

Her mother laughed too. Both of them seemed to understand that I imagined Bernadette and myself whirling around the room on gusts of metaphor.

We were all specifically permitted to wear civilian clothes to the dance. I owned none but had borrowed a red and gold tie which my father treasured, and my mother had dragged me off to Wynn's in Oxford Street at some stage and made me buy a brown sports coat which would now be of use but – she said – would see me off to university. If I was to become a great writer at an early age, I was unlikely to get much wear out of the thing, so I had ultimately let her choose which one. She too was amused as the Curran women had been. 'Aren't you interested in clothes at all? Your father loves them.'

Doomed Chatterton in a brown sports coat. Ahead of me the mystery of what the young women of the Dominican convent would look like in frocks, separated from the communal brown of their uniforms, differentiated by a hundred fabrics and dyes.

Mangan had earlier expressed an intention to wear his school uniform as a form of protest or a gesture that he didn't consider the event of much value. On the night it would look like an act of rebellion. But he didn't own street clothes anyhow, or need them, given where he was going.

At some point during the week before the dance, my mother told me that I would need to buy a corsage for Bernadette. Something put together by the staff of the florist shop round near Rossiter's newsagency. But what would they know of the particularity of my ardour, the particularity of the beauty of Bernadette Curran? On the way home from studying with Matt one night in Shortland Avenue, I paused by someone's spacious garden in Meredith Road, crammed as it was even in late autumn with a profusion of flowers, a bloom or two of which would not be missed. I reached over the brick fence and plucked a flower here, a flower there. White and violet and gold. The double-fronted brick of the bungalow belonging to the garden seemed to tolerate my act. It was like stealing a crust from a bakery. A venial sin of floral theft. Or was it even that, since within a few days a new bloom would appear where I had snipped with my thumb nail?

I got home late for dinner. I gave my mother the stolen flowers I had carried home negligently in my suit pocket.

She was appalled at first, but ultimately responded again in that half-amused way, which is one of the continuing mercies and follies of women. 'You could have been arrested,' she said. But restitution couldn't be made. 'No,' she said. 'Even if it were legal, these will look very meagre and mean. You'll have to spend money for once on a proper corsage.'

Flowers put together by the florist's plump hands? Instead of flowers stolen by moonlight by a poet?

Sometimes the world is too much with us though. So I gave in and went around to the florist and murmured under my artistic cowlick, 'I would like a corsage suitable for a young woman I am taking to a social event.'

The word *dance* died in my mouth. It was too poor a description and I didn't want this woman to think that I had wasted my time learning the steps. I would have preferred she thought I'd wasted my time *not* learning them.

On the night itself, I began the long ecstatic walk, carrying in my hand a cellophane corsage which now looked, even to me, like the night's suitable gesture. First I collected the Frawley girls in their flouncy skirts and altered by make-up. I had never seen that cosmetic shine on them before. They had not been allowed by Mr Frawley to go with a specific boy and so in a sense were under my care.

In Shortland Avenue Matt in his houndstooth sports jacket looked unfamiliar, like his own man, thundering eagerly up the hall, his snow white hair superbly combed. How had Mrs Tierney described his jacket to him. The Tierneys made a justifiable fuss of the Frawley girls in their frocks and transformed complexions. Matt's World War I veteran father, the Digger of Amiens into whose side the army doctors had poured their mercury, smiled with the most blatant fatherly pride.

Up the hill, past the oval to the Curran bungalow, waited Bernadette Curran, unutterably herself in a lavender and white dress.

My mother was correct about the corsage. Mrs Curran first of all was touched, she said, and impressed by it. The younger Currans queued to hold it in their shapely olive fingers. 'I wouldn't have expected this of you,' said Mrs Curran wonderingly.

I can remember little of the walk down Albert Street towards Homebush Road. Much must have been said, perhaps particularly by me. There was the yearning to hold her hand, of course, but the fear of the voltaic excess which would enter and overwhelm a person through such contact!

Now came the mass shock of seeing all the boys in their unfamiliar jackets and suits and ties standing around the steps of Strathfield Town Hall, peering out with brilliantined hair from the entryway. Some of them, like me and Matt, in the company of a girl or two. And all the dresses which made the girls strange and wonderful. Dresses bought as a result of consultations with mothers, or in defiance of them. There were a number of Brothers in the hall – Dinny McGahan, Brothers Markwell and Bryant supported by a constabulary of St Pat's and Santa Sabina parents. I don't think the Dominican nuns were there. It would have been contrary to the spirit of their rules. They were a serious-minded Order. They took 'solemn' vows, while the Christian Brothers took only 'simple' vows of poverty, chastity, and obedience.

Had Brother Bryant fortified himself out of the bottle under the chemistry benches for this night of gazing upon the expanses of young faces? I was too innocent and distracted to consider whether any Brother would find himself tempted by a sudden flash or perfect arm or waist. I wonder now did it haunt and/or delight any of them all the way back to their plain beds in the monastery on the corner of Edgar Street?

I danced with Bernadette, and made small talk, enchanted out of all attempts to be smart. The palms of her hands felt light and sweatless, and her fingers were long and narrow.

'Didn't you say you'd all taken lessons?' she asked, in impeccable step whenever I stumbled. But I was so delighted and feverish with the occasion, it didn't matter what was said. That she made sounds, that I did, was enough.

Next I danced with Rose Frawley, and with Denise. Rose plumper then Bernadette, Denise a little thinner than her. Great company, I thought. Both girls. Children of a brave father.

I got a sort of euphoria out of hooking my arm around these girls' waists, out of being aware of the touch of fabric and a sense of shape rather than of succulent flesh. I was aware, too, that my feelings towards the Frawley girls were almost fraternal, whereas my feelings for Bernadette were indefinable. Across the room, Freddie Ford held his mouth avidly, and in his eagerness danced with exaggerated steps. The girls he and others danced with tended as a group to remain calm, smiling in an arch way or casting their eyes up. I hoped I didn't look like Freddie. What was he wanting of the night? One of the Brothers had told us, 'Boys, if ever you get a girl in trouble, remember that it will always and forever be your fault. For girls aren't interested in human lust – they go along with the desires of males only out of generosity . . .'

In the occasional corner of a girl's face however could be seen something which didn't quite coincide with this belief.

We danced on in the last year of what could be called the past of dance. Within twelve months or so, rock and roll would arrive, and all dancing would become more pagan, more voluptuous and yet more solitary than it had been. Just the same, there was a certain pressure of ignorant desire, an unlettered yearning adequate for the year, in the town hall. I was astounded to see Freddie, no taller than me, dancing with the lankiest of the Santa Sabina girls, the one who was a champion high jumper. His head was tucked in under the balcony of her breasts. A chimpanzee nuzzling a gazelle. I wished he wouldn't do it.

The Frawley girls and I conducted an informal campaign to have dance partners approach Matt. Quite handsome enough for any girl in his houndstooth jacket.

Quite adequately gifted as a dancer after his serious lessons with Peter (Pog) O'Gallagher. Matt and Pog both had the air of men who were going to dance their way into women's affections, and it should have been no hardship for any girl to dance with Matt. Looking around the room for likely partners for him, I saw a fine-featured, dark-haired girl, whose face I remembered. Yes, the year before. I'd played for the St Pat's eight-stone Rugby League Team against De La Salle College Ashfield, in their blue and white horizontal-striped guernseys. Brother Markwell played me in the second row but gave me instructions to break quickly from the scrum, like a break-away in Rugby Union. I did that, and if the half-back or five-eighth had made a break, they could pass the ball back infield to me.

My opposite number in the De La Salle scrum had the same face as this girl – indeed was her twin. She had been watching the game with some other Santa Sabina girls from the seats in front of the Stockade. And now here were her own features but in her brother's face, emerging from the scrum to stop me.

That day I had seen unnecessary tentativeness in the male twin's face. I stepped on my right foot, brushed through his tackle and palmed him off by the shoulder. Wonderful because such things happened so rarely in my sporting life but had been regularly dreamed of since I was an infant. I scored a try from that position, standing up the fullback too with another step off the right foot. A glorious day. I still remember *knowing* the other team and especially the twin were not equipped for me. I felt both arrogance and guilt at having got past him so easily. What would it do to the girl's view of her brother?

Now the same girl, unforgettable exactly because I remembered every nuance of her brother's bewildered features as they came up towards me, was standing at the side of the room in a frock somewhat like Bernadette

Curran's. Someone as beautiful as that must also have nobility. That's what the Romantics said. You could read it in the features.

I went up to her. I introduced myself. 'I just wondered if you'd like to dance with our friend Matt there.'

Some look of panic at once entered her lovely face. Some passion for safety I'd seen in her brother's features as he decided he would not expend too much pain on stopping me.

'No, no.' She made no excuses. She turned away. She had gone pale.

I went back to robust Rose Frawley, and pointed the girl out. 'Oh, she's so bloody stuck-up they need a ladder to get her down,' said Rose.

But I noticed across the room, past Freddie nuzzling in under the mammaries of the high jumper, that the black-haired girl was pale, solitary, abashed. Her own timidity shamed her. I felt a strange sorrow, a kind of brotherly pity. Quickly diffused by dancing again with fragrant Bernadette Curran, and feeling the fabric crinkling against my wrist.

'You've left that poetry book at home,' she said. 'At last.'

But I knew she didn't mean that.

Of all those who danced with Matt, the Frawleys and Bernadette were best. They knew he was just another boy. They knew he liked girls. He would ask me to describe the colour of the dresses. Terms like white and red and blue meant something to him in a sort of verbal context he had got from his reading. I had once quizzed him, when we strolled down Broughton Road, why he so often asked about colours, and what he got out of it when I said the word *red*.

'I imagine that must be pretty rich,' he told me.

Another time – I think we might have been a bit older than we were the night of the dance – he said, 'I know red's different than blue and white. It's like difference in sounds. You find some sounds are red and green, and others blue or white. *Red* is a red sound.'

So he would ask me that night, 'What colour is Denise Frawley's dress, Mick?'

The Frawleys and Bernadette danced with Matt as with a real, young male whose ideas had equal and democratic weight with everyone else's. Other girls seemed too scared to converse with him and might panic in midstep and hold him at severe arm's length like a patient, even like someone contagious. Such treatment is one of the griefs of the blind, and Matt could tell when it happened, the subtle brand of terror which is only an inch away from abhorrence.

It was a good night for him though. His snow-white face went pink with the success of the dancing. He was better than me, except for the injustice that I could see myself being clumsy.

The evening turned out to be a late one by the standards of Strathfield, all of ten-thirty before we found ourselves on the street again. On the way home, I told myself I would hold Bernadette Curran's hand to her satisfaction and mine. I would evaporate at the touch, dissolving into some great metaphorical ether.

But in Albert Road, as we strolled along, our splendours barely used up, Mangan having not danced a single time and now lagging behind and humming Mahler to himself, Curran's corsage still fresh, I tried to slip my hand into hers and was rebuffed.

I asked why. She said, 'Why out of all the hands do you have to hold mine? Hold Denise's.' The quieter Frawley sister.

'What's the matter with you?' she asked loudly at one stage, when I made a second stealthy attempt. I felt foolish but still savoured the long walk to Curran's place, the furthest of all our houses from the Town

Hall. Yet this stroll beneath the box trees, past the oval where I had been in the rare position of athletically embarrassing the twin brother of the dark-haired girl, came to a close inconclusively. We drank tea at the Currans' and answered Mr and Mrs Curran's questions about who danced with whom, and I had not vaporized yet but was still on earth and indeed needed to use the urinal. Oh ever wakeful, ever abashing flesh! But I could not attend to the need at the Currans'. To enter their bathroom would be to declare too frankly my humanity and to discover unwanted news about theirs.

I would wait until I dropped Matt off at his house in Shortland Road. Both his parents were waiting up.

'How did he go?' genial Mr Tierney asked me.

'You know Matt,' I said so that he could hear. 'He's a tiger. He couldn't knock them off with sticks. Everyone fell for him. He's ruthless with women. He tells them such lies, etc., etc., etc.'

We all laughed like drains with and at Matt the ladykiller. Yet the Tierney parents knew well enough. There were dark-haired girls, or red-haired, or auburn or fair who would not dance with him. There always would be.

I was able to sneak into their toilet. They were used to the idea that even Mangan and I had bladders.

Then the final leg of the delivery – taking the Frawley girls to their place. Mangan too went off languidly yawning. For geographic reasons, I always walked the longest. In one sense I took the greatest pains with my friends, in another I took the longest comfort from them. There was an end-of-the-evening flatness to the conversation with Rose and Denise.

'Did you see Freddie? What a bloody brute!'

'Mick, why won't you and Mangan learn to dance?' asked innocent Denise.

'I don't intend to need it,' I told her.

'Well,' said Denise, 'Rose may not need it either, but she's learned.'

'Why wouldn't Rose need it?'

Rose got a smooth smile on her face. It was a form of pride I had seen once or twice before. I had seen it in Dahdah the year before.

'You're not trying to say you're going to join the Dominicans?' I asked. It was an astonishing guess. For Rose was the earthy one. She picked her ears for wax. She said *bloody* and *drongo*. She lacked any nun-like gravity.

'She might very well be,' said Denise.

'There aren't enough good-looking blokes around,' said Rose, and laughed at me as was her custom.

I would hear from a number of sources versions of what had happened, of how the signs, the command, the *vocation* had dipped down and brushed Rose Frawley with its wing. Up at Saint Lucy's School for the Blind, from which Matt and an accomplice had once tried to escape, there was a somewhat plump old nun called Mother Margaret. One day earlier in the year when a dramatic Sydney storm, all thunderhead, lightning and raindrops as big as thumbs, descended on Strathfield, she had gone to the nuns' bathroom to close the window. She had stood on the bath to do so, had slipped, fallen into the bath and broken her leg. Her cries brought some of the other nuns in. When they tried to lift her out of the enamel tub, she screamed with pain. It looked to the younger nuns as if her hip of leg were broken. They wanted to call Dr Buckley of Homebush, the doctor who looked like Bing Crosby and tended to the nuns on a Love-of-God basis. Mother Margaret forbade them to telephone him. 'I don't want any man to see me with my legs in the air,' she told the other nuns. (This was reported to me by Mrs Frawley.)

The nuns disobeyed her only when the poor thing lost consciousness. It *was* a broken leg and not long thereafter she developed pneumonia. One afternoon in her ultimate convalescence, she told Mrs Frawley, who visited St Lucy's regularly to do odd jobs for the nuns, that she wanted to see Rose. The Frawley girls were frequently up at Saint Lucy's anyhow running errands for the nuns through an arrangement made between the convent and Mr Frawley.

So Rose went up to see Mother Margaret.

Margaret told her that while she thought through God's mercy and the kindness of His Blessed Mother she might survive this illness, the accident was her *memento mori*, a reminder that her time on earth would be henceforth quite short. Had Rose ever thought of becoming a Dominican nun? And if she had, would she now consider carrying on Margaret's name by taking it as her religious name when she uttered her Solemn Vows?

'You see,' my mother told my father one night, 'they don't have children, so it's important for them to think of their religious name going on.'

Maternity would out.

Naturally, I now looked at Rose as a girl-woman transformed and elevated. The spirit listeth where it will, but I had never expected it to listeth towards Rose.

Some time soon after the news of Rose got out, I met Mr Crespi, the Italian door-to-door Watson's salesman, the Red, one morning in Meredith Street.

'My young friend,' he said. He looked grey and irritable and smelled of tobacco. 'I hear of them putting the hard word on that poor girl. This is a criminal act, young man. Why do you all stand around in such slavery? Why are parents so ready to sacrifice their young?'

'The Frawleys see it in a different light,' I told him, a

little angered. The Frawleys didn't seem like dupes to me, though they were temperamental volunteers, both Rose and Mr Frawley.

'What different light?' he asked me. 'This is a new country. It is therefore meant to be a country of fresh ideas, of revolutionary energy. I see none of that. I see only bowing of the head to Mr Church and Mr Bank and Mr Labor Party. That's why there will never be a true socialist government in this country.'

I knew from my father that Mrs Talbot's Left faction had been voted out of the Strathfield branch of the Labor Party by a mass of industrial groupers.

I enquired how Mrs Talbot was these days. 'Consumption is no holiday,' he told me as if I wilfully thought it was easier than revolution. 'They're saying she must go into Bodington.'

This was a famous sanatarium in the Blue Mountains.

'The doctors overcharge,' he told me. 'This does not happen in genuine democracy.'

I had said I would write to her, since she had often talked to me when I passed the boarding house as a child. And I did remember to write a note that night, a letter in which I quoted GMH's poem *Now Time's Andromeda*. I wonder what she made of it.

Now Crespi went on his way with his bag of unguents and disinfectants.

'Do something for that girl,' he said over his shoulder. 'Introduce her to life.'

But I had already. I'd read her snatches of Eliot and GMH.

I could have told him too that the *calling* of Rose was the most dramatic thing to have happened to the Frawleys since the Potato Famine. It was the stuff of novels. Young flesh which would never be touched with anything but spirit – it was more dramatic than flesh that was going to take the conventional way. Primp itself up, go out in cars, end up disgruntled in hair curlers.

We paid for the vanities of the Strathfield Town Hall dance. As we all took for granted, Brother Dinny McGahan was a good fellow. But we also understood that in his world and ours, there were two enemies. The lesser was secularism and the greater was sex.

In the matter of secularism, the Brothers warned us that at Sydney University there was a famous humanist professor, a Logical Positivist called Anderson. Seductive as Satan, riddled with secularism, contemptuous of the philosophy and theology of Saint Thomas Aquinas, the whole great edifice called Thomism.

Former students of St Pat's had told Dinny and Buster of Anderson. Now someone, a parent perhaps, a Santa Sabina nun informed by a Santa Sabina prefect, told them of the other and closer peril. Sex. Especially sex and Freddie Ford.

Ford was stood up in class on account of his crazed dancing with the high jumper and admonished by Dinny in terms which he would probably remember all his life. 'You are too vain, sir . . . ah . . . and impurity lies beyond vanity, waiting to spring. You took a girl by the waist purely for impure gratification. Did you think of her mother? Ah . . . did you think of the Virgin Mary looking down on you? Did you think of your own mother and the peril to your immortal soul?'

There's no doubting the anguish Brother McGahan demonstrated that day. We were his charges and he had permitted us to be led into the garden of temptation, the lushness at Strathfield Town Hall.

Catholicism's huge fear of sexuality, its morbid panic,

its detestation of most sins of the flesh (including masturbation, of which I was uninformed at that time), was at play in him. He was both the victim and promoter of that awful phobia.

Freddie went out weeping, a rare phenomenon amongst sixteen-year-olds. He was suspended from school pending his possible expulsion. The rest of us were set to write a confession of what we had done and what we observed others to have done during the dance. Dinny bade us write the truth under pain of conscience.

The unknowing might think that he meant to take these accounts off and get some perverse pleasure from them. Brother McGahan was in this matter though not perverse but tormented. He was concerned to find how far the rot had gone. He was concerned to lay God's preventive axe to the root of the tree.

Only Matt was not required to set to work on this. His Braille typewriter would have punched out confessions that no one other than he could read. As we wrote, a red pall of shame hung in the room. I'm sure there were some brave, democratic, even Godless souls who were not intimidated by it. I confess I wasn't one of them.

The truth is, all of us, the ethos of the place and time, were what would be called Jansenist, though we were ignorant of the term.

As I would learn later, Jansen was a Bishop of Ypres, the town in Flanders for which Mr Tierney and Digger Crichton had fought. Jansen had argued the utter incapacity of decent people to choose to obey moral law, particularly to overcome their own concupiscence. He must have been faced by phenomena such as Freddie's lust for the Santa Sabina high jumper. Only Divine Grace could save you from the flesh, according to Bishop Jansen.

Jansen's propositions were ultimately condemned by the Vatican since they seemed to undermine the doctrine of free will. He died in 1640, but his doctrine about grace, and his high stress on the essential and continual austerity which must be applied in matters of sexual morality lived on at the Convent of Port Royal in Paris. Here it attracted a number of famous adherents including Blaise Pascal, the prodigy, mathematician and author of the *Pensées*.

Not knowing at that stage about Pascal's Jansenist and therefore heretical connections, I was already dipping into the *Pensées*, and was particularly attracted of course, as others were, by the aphorism, 'The heart has its reasons which reason cannot understand.' This *pensée* seemed to fit in very well with my feelings at the Santa Sabina dance. Reason could not have gone close to expressing the impulses which led me to grope for the divine Curran's hand.

The French and the Vatican found it very hard to suppress Jansenism, and in fact many Irish priests, exiled from their country by the British Penal Laws, ingested Jansenism while studying in France. Every heresy, it stands to reason, adds its stain to the chief, central orthodoxy. The panic that grace would run out and that flesh would conquer, that will and spirit were not enough – that was the Jansenist panic which infected Fifth Year Blue and its popular teacher on the corner of Edgar Street in the antipodes in 1952.

Perhaps by explaining this theological background, I am trying to explain to the reader how I wrote what I did. 'I did hear one boy say that it was wonderful to get up against a girl's breasts.' (Freddie had in fact said this to Matt and me in passing.) 'When I was walking home myself, I made a number of stupid attempts to hold a girl's hand. Although this was a minor matter, I understand how it could have led to something worse . . .'

Something worse? Small chance. With me a Celestial, and Curran a sensible and determined refuser of my hand.

As I wrote, Matt's Braille typewriter keys *did* begin

to crunch away at the heavy, brown cartridge paper onto which he habitually put everything he knew – the dynasties of Egypt, the Athenian Republic, the Punic Wars, and whatever he felt when he touched the few peculiar, feminine fabrics which encased the Frawleys and Curran, and smelled their scents. What he was writing though was his business.

I heard from the Frawley girls that there was a similar outrage shown by the Dominican nuns, who had heard reports from some of the girls' parents about the way their daughters had been clasped, hugged, caressed. Mother Concordia, the oldest surviving Irishwoman from the first group of Dominicans who came to Strathfield, a sort of Matriarch Emeritus of Santa Sabina, took all the fourth and fifth year girls to the chapel, where they said one decade of the Rosary to confirm them in the virtues of Catholic womanhood.

Hearing the Frawley girls utter the name, I felt a certain awe that Concordia had been put into commission. I had known this nun when I was very young, during the war – when we came down from the bush and I was sent to the little Dominican school of Saint Martha's. Here we had occasional, august visits from Concordia, and these deepened the dread I already had of the school.

I was not happy there to start with – not very bright, easily distracted, easily contracting a wheeze. Running around in the playground made my nose stream, but I lost my handkerchief readily, and the wrists of my navy blue blazer became marred by the snail-like silvery traces of mucus.

The young, impeccable Bernadette Curran had been a member of the same class. She never spilled ink, and her nose never ran. One day on the way down Homebush Road towards the bus, she asked me, 'Why do you always have drippings on your work?'

I burned, and said, 'I don't see any dripping around here.'

But she had noticed my terrible weakness. In the subjectivity of childhood misery, every day was a month and every week a year, and both the ink and my nose flowed without spate. To make up for the runniness of my nasal passage, I tried to be a lad with the other lads. When someone started pissing contests up the creosoted walls of Saint Martha's boys' toilet I joined in enthusiastically, straining my lower belly to get my stream of urine an inch higher than that of the bloke beside me.

This was the year in which Singapore had fallen to the Japanese and the occasional Japanese reconnaissance plane went over Sydney, the year in which the entire Australian world scheme – development as a working man's utopia under the umbrella of Imperial power – had been disrupted by the humiliation of British and Australian arms. Yet it was our urinary crimes which seemed to cry to the heavens, and evoked a visit from Santa Sabina to Saint Martha's by Mother Concordia. She got all the boys from the Infants and First Grade and took us into the boys' toilet, aligning us in threes between the urinal stalls.

She was a big-boned woman, though I didn't think of her in those terms then. I thought of her as being constructed of one piece through and through, legless as a mountain. Divine thunder was compacted into her eyes and the strip of brow we could see below her celluloid brow-piece. She had a long, immaculate stick of chalk in her hand. She reached into the urinal stalls and drew a line about two feet three inches off the ground.

She moved from stall to stall, continuing the line. The stick of chalk did not break in her hand, despite the unevenness of the tarred and creosoted walls. She worked down the left side of the stalls and then passed across the rear of our silent column and worked on the facing right wall. It was awesome to see her mark and measure this infant, male place. When she had finished her work, she was panting slightly, pursing her lips, and she stood in front of us. The chalk was evenly worn down – she had taken lessons long ago in stopping it cracking and wearing to a point.

She said, 'I know what you've been doing to your shame. Think of what your dear mothers would say. You have disgraced them. More importantly, you have wounded our Saviour and appalled His Blessed Mother. I tell you this: see that mark on the wall. Any boy who piddles above that mark will attract the anger of dear God and cause His Blessed Mother to shed tears of shame.'

She then took an eighteen inch ruler from a deep, deep pocket in her habit, called forth two of the ringleaders – someone must have talked – and gave them three on each hand. I don't think it hurt hugely, but its intimation of the Deity's lightning bolts caused both boys to weep.

A few weeks later, the Americans and the Australians stopped a large Japanese convoy in the Coral Sea, and then a few months after that – thirty miles from Port Moresby – the Diggers stopped the Japanese advance across New Guinea. All so that we should grow up in freedom, except the freedom to pee above the line.

Ten years later we had again failed to keep our unregenerative selves in order in the boys' lavatory at St Martha's, and Concordia had been forced to come out of ever deeper retirement to lead the girls of Santa Sabina in prayers for our redemption.

We waited to receive exemplary punishments for our behaviour at the dance, but the only penalty that was imposed was the most obvious – there would be no dance the following year. A saner system might have imposed a different penalty altogether – a compulsory monthly dance, something to de-mystify women and prepare us to be fit lovers and husbands. But I believed at the time that we sixteen-year-old victims of Jansen were getting what we deserved. I deserved it for trying to take Bernadette Curran's hand so importunately. Everyone else deserved it for his own shameful reason. Shame, in fact, was inescapable. Every man was a liar and a luster. If *then* I had been given the choice for life between producing children through passion and explicit sexual feeling, or producing them merely by reading GMH to one's beloved – I have to confess that under those particular prevailing winds I would have chosen the latter.

V

Mystical, penitential, angular Father Byrne was moved out of Strathfield parish to Lewisham, six stops closer to Sydney down the Western Line. Many said they were going to follow him there for Sunday Mass, since he said Mass like a saint, and Monsignor Loane said it like an accountant. I was not aware though that anyone really took the trouble of catching the train to Lewisham for that purpose. Uttering the idea itself stood as an adequate statement of discontent at Father Byrne's being moved by the Cardinal to another parish.

Father Byrne himself would have frowned on the cult of personality. Amongst his new jobs, he told all of us boys on the next vocation-hunting safari to St Pat's, was chaplaincy of the nearby Little Company of Mary Hospital. I knew the hospital well. I had my tonsils out there, in a room of other etherized children. Fighting against the ether swab, waking weakened, succumbing to pneumonia, and being nursed by a tall Irish nun in white and blue. It was easy to imagine Father Byrne keeping a vigil for sick children, sick women, or bringing around at their last gasp decayed, agnostic old men.

Father Byrne was on the front line in another sense too. Lewisham Hospital was a prime target for Campbell's Raiders. Every night now, Mr Frawley told me on one of my visits to the house, two men kept watch in the convent garden armed with lengths of pipe or cricket bats. The nuns had the number of the meat wholesaler in Homebush who could gather a flying squad of six or eight groupers to come to the convent's rescue within a quarter of an hour.

On a further visit to Saint Pat's, Father Byrne – talking to Fifth Year as a whole – asked us to pray for a particular patient at Lewisham Hospital. She was a girl from the bush. She'd had an ulcer grow on her leg and it had entered the bone. Her future did not look good. Only eighteen years old, but very bitter! She said the usual things – nuns were cruel; the Pope claimed to be infallible, but if so why couldn't he pick the winner of the Melbourne Cup. And she didn't believe in life after death. She was pleasant enough apart from that, and let him pray with her sometimes. She showed no awareness, he said, of the mortal peril of her soul.

I suppose that some of us, told of this dark, tragic girl from the bush, whose shinbone had grown cancerous, imagined how we might with our Fix-a-Flexed hairdos and our crooked smiles bring her around. Even morbidly imagined – since such scenes were part of the mythology of our upbringing – her dying grateful, going beautiful to God with our names on her lips.

People became aware that Father Byrne was travelling broadly throughout the Western suburbs of Sydney, garnering prayers for this poor doomed girl. My mother heard about it in a sermon Father Byrne gave at Benediction. Every supporter of Father Byrne between Stanmore and Granville was praying for the girl from the bush with the cancerous leg.

At the beginning of the Sydney winter, when I was working on the Newman essay and making up my mind whether to try for the Firsts and Seconds Rugby League team or keep a divine distance, it was announced that Father Byrne was coming back to Strathfield parish to say a special Mass of thanks. For his patient had not only returned to the faith, but had been astoundingly cured! St Martha's Church was packed for the event. It was nearly as big as a basilica anyhow, and distinguished by a huge mural of the Assumption of the Virgin Mary in the half-dome behind the high altar. People came to be uplifted and challenged by the news, to hear Father Byrne's sonorous Latin. My father liked priests who got into the Mass, sliced through the litany like a buzz saw and let him out after forty minutes. But I, like Father Byrne, was a lover of sonorous Latin. I attended this Mass with my mother, making the long walk up Homebush Road.

We noticed that in the front row sat a young woman, pleasant-faced, dressed in a blue blouse, white skirt and white cardigan. Her leg was bandaged and she smiled a lot. She was obviously the redeemed girl. As Father Byrne said in his sermon, not referring to her by name or gesture as she tilted her face ecstatically towards the pulpit, her bone cancer had disappeared, and the wound left by the ulcer was clean and was healing even as we spoke.

Outside afterwards, talking to Mangan and the Frawleys, we saw her emerge, helped along by the middle-aged woman who had sat beside her. People did not talk to her, and some looked bleakly at her, almost in the way the ignorant looked at Matt. Her miraculous cure made her an outsider as well as a wonder. Homebush Road nonetheless brimmed with miraculous hope. With a faint limp, and in the company of her middle-aged attendant, she moved off in the direction of Strathfield Station to catch the train back to Lewisham. There, everyone seemed to know, she was living in the hospital but praying with the novices. It was now near certain that her life was mapped out.

I must say again, lest this sound too much like the account of some sect even more frantic than we were, that there was a lot of pity for people who were as God-marked as Father Byrne and this girl. No one except lunatics like myself wanted to have these experiences.

They were out of kilter with the sunny suburb, at odds with the *genius loci* of Homebush/Strathfield on the edge of the age of Rock and Roll.

Mr Frawley, who knew people close to Father Byrne in Lewisham Parish, who had also been close to him in Strathfield, later told us a gloss on the tale. Late one night, just before the recovery of the girl from the bush became known, while Father Byrne prayed in Saint Thomas's Lewisham, in a church long vacated by his more worldly colleagues, he had actually suffered a vision of the Virgin Mary. Once more, a mixed blessing in itself. The officials of the Church did not approve of visions and treated them with extreme scepticism. They put a burden of proof on the person claiming to have witnessed them, subjected them to all manner of tests and examinations, suspected them of demonic possession. And all this before such psychiatric terms as *hysteria* or *schizophrenia* had come into common usage in the church; that is, long before Freud's breath was felt on conventional Catholic orthodoxy.

Mr Frawley himself pitied Father Byrne the way people pity a lone polar explorer who perishes of his vision. In that, again Mr Frawley was not at all like a member of a charismatic sect, who having seen others talk in tongues *wants* to talk in tongues himself.

Father Byrne was now under as much suspicion as eccentric Monsignor Leonard, who came to Strathfield sometimes to say Mass and who gave away his shoes or his coat to vagrants or dipsos. Christ's counsels in this regard were in most people's minds not designed for literal interpretation in Homebush Road. A baroque extreme of vision in a non-Italianate locale – that was the inherent problem of what Father Byrne had seen.

At the very time of his vision, the sleeping girl from the bush woke up in the nearby hospital with a new feeling of well-being, and called the night sister, a nun who looked at the dressings and became a witness to the sudden, unexplained remission the girl was now in. The wound amazingly gone!

This remarkable, imagination-hijacking event nonetheless needed to share the early Sydney winter with other questions. The question for example of Rugby League. At St Pat's – as already intimated – we played *rugby-à-treize*, thirteen-a-side Rugby League, which in Eastern Australia was the chief game and which was largely our map of heroism and the universe. Running with and passing bladders filled with air to teammates was to sport what GMH was to poetry, what Bernadette Curran was to ethereal beauty. The Brothers taught us to play splendidly; lightning backline movements, determined forwards. St Pat's teams were always bringing back State Championships from the August knock-out competitions at the Sydney Cricket Ground. I had participated in one such victory the year before, in a team coached by Brother Markwell, a lean Queenslander who tended to admire the industrial groupers.

In the eight-stone team – that is, the one hundred and twelve pound weight limit – we had been sublimely schooled and disciplined. The ball rattled out along the back line into the hands of a boy centre who would later play for the Australian national Rugby team, the Wallabies. Then, after drawing his man, that is, sucking in the defender and committing him to a tackle, the future Wallaby would give it to our winger, who was a future Commonwealth Games sprinter.

We had played the game which qualified us for the final on the prodigiously sacred turf of the Sydney Cricket Ground, and then had beaten a Marist Brothers team on the Sydney Cricket Ground Number Two, winning the trophy by a single try. This was a wilder success than I'd ever imagined in my asthma-ridden pre-pubescence.

Now – at the beginning of a new season – I was all set up to try out for halfback or five-eighth (the English called if fly-half) for the First XIII.

My father had been a great five-eighth on the Northern Rivers of New South Wales. Late into my manhood, old gents with sun cancers on their faces would come up to me and tell me how good he had been. One of them once said, 'He was one of the best five-eighths I ever saw, but he used to come the knuckle.' He had a reputation for putting in punches on the blind side, safe from the referee's gaze. He was always a fiery man, and even much later in his old age, walking with a stick, was willing to take on people who offended him. Willing to *come the knuckle.*

My father had played in four premiership teams for Taree Old Bar Rugby League Club, an awesome outfit in the bush in the 1930s, one that was not beyond stacking its team with famous visiting players from Sydney, offering them an introduction to the local girls and a skinful of beer. He also played for Central Kempsey. Once, when his Irish mother was very ill, his sisters had asked him not to play, but he had anyhow and dislocated his collarbone. He hid the fact from them and carried the injury untreated. In my childhood he still carried a strange socket in his collarbone, from a peculiar way the bones settled themselves.

The trial for the First XIII was to be played on the oval itself, before interested spectators – parents, brothers, the occasional exquisite Santa Sabina girl. Curran came down for games on the oval on a Sunday afternoon – it was only a three hundred yard walk from the bungalow where the Curran women stored their beauty and cleverness.

My father had been so proud of me approximating his earlier competence in the game that in the past few years he often invited his cousin Pat, who was the family's success, a graduate of Sydney University and a lawyer in the western suburb of Granville, to see me play.

As the Christian Brothers of Ireland had made a long journey to Australia, so had this Northern English game, Rugby League. In Huddersfield, Yorkshire in 1893, a number of interested parties had separated away from the Rugby Union, which we liked to call with inverse snobbery 'the gentlemen's and dilettantes' game', and formed a new league which enabled workers from the mine and the mill to be paid for the time they lost in playing the game, and to be compensated for injury. It took more than a decade for League to move on to Sydney, where the great Test batsman, Victor Trumper, was one of its earliest promoters. In eastern Australia the teams which went over to Rugby League became the most popular, crowd-pulling teams. Rugby League remained a working-class, Christian Brothers sort of game. The grammar schools which were an imitation of Eton and Harrow, and the Jesuit Schools which imitated Stonyhurst, played the original Rugby, the fifteen-men-a-side game, itself a marvellous version of football too and one I would later come to love with almost equal passion.

This evolution and social context of the game of Rugby League led to my running onto the oval on a given Sunday, wearing a jersey of black and white hoops, convinced of the significance of what I was doing and observed by my hopeful father and his cousin Pat.

I found it hard to get going in that game. I had a sense that my tackling was more than adequate, but I felt leaden-footed in attack. Brother Markwell had taught me to watch the direction people's legs were stepping – in talented footballers, a step off the right or left foot could take the hips away from where you were sure they were. Due to this training, I brought some big lads down but didn't make much headway when I had the ball, and despite my best efforts, didn't often get near the ball either.

A Freudian would say that I was awed by the presence of these two old warriors, my father and Pat.

After the game, Dinny McGahan told me that he would start me at five-eighth in the Thirds just for the moment. He was sure that I could work my way up to the Seconds if I got back some of my form of the previous year. Walking home by the normal long route – Matt's, the Frawleys', orating, referring to poetry, discussing Graham Greene's new novel *The Heart of the Matter* with Mr Frawley – I was near to making up my mind not to bother playing this climactic year. It was partly vanity – the ignominy of starting in the Thirds. But there was wisdom to it also. I was busy enough. My companionship with Matt already kept me occupied. I could claim resurgent asthma, from which I had been thankfully free for the past four years. Each of the Brothers knew it had been the curse of my earlier adolescence, and that I had very nearly died from a bout of it in Kempsey at the age of five.

The next day I approached Dinny McGahan and told him the lie. He who had introduced me to the history of Fascism, to the *Anschluss*, to the courses of World War I and World War II.

'Brother,' I said (I'd given up the diminutive 'Bra' commonly used by younger boys and by the farting-and-innuendo crowd), 'I think I'd better miss Rugby League this year. I've got the asthma coming back.'

I may even have quoted Dr Buckley, our local physician, who had brought me out of earlier attacks and spoken calmly to my mother. Since Buckley treated the Brothers and the nuns for free, his name operated as an impeccable medical authority.

I would regret not having the humility to play in the Thirds. All my life I have retained a curiosity about whether I would have been good enough for the Seconds or even the Firsts. The Seconds were pretty good players after all.

In any case my winter was now clear. I had no excuse for not by year's end writing poetry as sublime as GMH's, no excuse for not training with Matt until he was ready to run against boys his own age for not or achieving some other form of transcendence.

Sleek Monsignor Loane was enraged by the very book Mr Frawley and I had already discussed. *The Heart of the Matter* was doing great business and even Pelligrini's Devotional Bookseller had it on sale. Monsignor Loane and other parish priests would quickly enough give it a bad reputation.

'It has nothing,' said Monsignor Loane from his pulpit, 'no merits in terms of plot comparable say to the great Sir Walter Scott or Charles Dickens. The concerns of its central character, a British District Officer in an African colony, seem to be predominantly to do with fornication and the destruction of a Catholic marriage. This *novel* holds out an apparently theologically sound theory that even the soul bent on self-destruction can be redeemed in the last seconds of its existence. The fact remains that God extends his mercy only to those who have shown good will at some point of their lives, and not to a man like this District Officer who shows nothing but callousness at every stage. This book exploits the concept of redemption and sanctifying grace as if it were a party trick. I urge all parishioners under conscience to advise their families and friends against its seductive argument. The new edition of the life of Saint Therese of Lisieux makes better and more valid reading.'

'But I've already read the Greene book,' I said to Mangan and the Frawley girls outside.

'Well, of course you have,' said Rose Frawley.

'You can't be scrupulous about it,' Mangan advised me, laying his bright brown medieval eyes upon me. Perhaps he saw that I already had the beginnings of a neurotic scrupulousness.

I think they all knew that I had the makings of a possible zealot. In a remote city, in a former colony not yet fully recovered from colonial status, I feared I had caused some lesion in the universe by reading a book condemned by Monsignor Loane, a priest whom – unlike Father Byrne – I didn't particularly respect. For a second in that sun-drenched year so rich with promise, I suddenly feared the loss of myself through the reading of the book, exactly the way GMH feared the loss of himself if the huge grandeur of his poetry were released on the world. He didn't want his poems on his slate when he faced the great cosmic sifting.

Graham Greene had succumbed to a typical and blessed writer's temptation of writing about the mysteries of mercy as they bore on the souls of the weak, the venal, the concupiscent. According to the Monsignor, while pretending to be devoutly Catholic, Greene was tainted with secularism, with the adoration of the things of the age – science preferred to theology, modernism preferred over works of the Fathers of the Church, and repentance after fornication preferred to chastity.

The Church made it all very hard for writers and readers, if you took its edicts literally. The Vatican had its Index of Prohibited Works which included such apparently harmless tales as Alexander Dumas' *The Three Musketeers*, on the list presumably because of its bias against Cardinal Richelieu and its romanticizing of duelling. Secularism was everywhere, and those books in which it was presented had the immediate honour of being put on the Index.

The next Saturday night I went up to St Martha's again, entered the confessional and confessed, not to Monsignor Loane but to the curate, that I had read a Graham Greene novel. I knew it was no grave matter but couldn't help confessing it, as if behind my exultance in life lay a thin-lipped fanatic. 'That's not necessarily a bad thing,' he said. 'It's a Christian duty to inform yourself, as long as you balance it with devotional reading to protect yourself mentally from some of the things portrayed.'

The priest was probably wondering why I didn't confess the normal things, the lusts and masturbations. But Celestials didn't go in for that sort of thing.

It was wonderful always to come out of the confessional, having told the truth, irrespective of whether the embarrassing announcement were the reading of Graham Greene or the inchoate desiring of a girl. James Joyce had written definitively on the exaltation of a *good* confession, the internal horror of a *bad* one. How joyful the long, treading-on-air walk down Homebush Road, the readiness with which Hopkinsesque imagery sprang to mind in the immaculate soul.

Sometimes Matt came to St Martha's wanting to confess. I would take him to the door of the confessional, guide him down on to the little kneeler by the grille, and close the door behind him. The doors of the confessionals of Strathfield were designed to click shut on ball-bearing locks, and so they were a mixture of the latest fittings and the most ancient Sacrament.

Returning to a pew to wait until Matt was finished, I would notice the edification on the faces of the elderly women saying their pre-confessional prayers and waiting their turn. I wondered what Matt had to confess, in his colourless world. What sensuality, in what form, broke into his darkness? How did he speak of his desires? Was it touch Matt confessed? A touch of silk dress and of waist succulently remembered from the St Pat's–Santa Sabina dance? Mysteries none of us discussed. Even Mangan and I, in our florid egotisms, in our striving for the dazzling word. I did sometimes wonder even then whether Matt ever confessed that I got on his nerves, as I must have sometimes in my freneticism and vanities.

On top of that we had of course been frequently instructed that confession was not for criminals. Virtue was maintained by frequent confession. Perhaps as well as confessing the standard sins, Matt was storing up credits. I'm sure the sentimental clients of the confessional, who understood blindness even less than I, must have thought so.

The hearing of confessions always seemed an august task for a priest to undertake on Saturday afternoons and nights. I'd been told of priests who were punters and who took the new portable radios into the confessional with them so that they could hear race results between penitents. But I could not imagine anyone so far under-awed as that by the power to bind and to loose. The old bigot rumour was that priests got indecent thrills listening to people's sexual admissions. But I couldn't imagine anything garish being confessed by the staid parishioners of St Martha's.

❦❦❦

And in the spirit of these reflections on the power of priests to bind and loose, Father Byrne was back, seeing if I had yet decided whether I had been called to the priesthood. I had a sense of him as a man for whom at the Virgin's behest a miracle had been worked. Therefore

I did not dare to lie to him lest I be fixed by his scarifying gaze.

'I find that I still lack certainty,' I told him. Indeed, I still had my eye on Sydney University, I preferred that option. As I spoke, I noticed his cheeks. They seemed hollowed by the drag within him. The drag of weariness, and the gravity of all the half-truths people told him. But he had his stratagems too.

'There is a vocations' day at the major seminary at Manly,' he said. 'A number of boys from St Pat's are going over there on Sunday week. One of the deacons will show you around the place and answer your questions. Do you think you would like to go?'

I felt that I had to agree. The only way I could think of to avoid it was to get a divine flash which told me at that instant I shouldn't think about becoming a priest. I felt uneasy about being an impostor though, since in the end I would have to announce to him that I was staying in the world with Curran, going to university and glory. Vanity which had got me into this pretence would in the end have to be paid for with the shame of being seen through by Father Byrne's mystic eye. He would then know yet again that his supposed disciples played on his innocence.

The weariness I noticed in him that early winter day might have been a foreshadowing of events that were about to occur in Lewisham Hospital – involving Campbell of *The Rock*.

I think of the nights of those boyhood winters as dark, even though they were by the standards of other hemispheres relatively mild. No night life graced the Western Line. The hotels closed at six so that even the drunks went home early. Mangan and I might be found walking the streets, discussing the suppression of the Kulaks by Stalin, or the confessions of St Augustine, or T. S. Eliot. A scatter of people attended the cinema in Parramatta Road, though there was a sense that going to the pictures on a week night was a bit like drinking in the morning. Everyone else was at home listening to the radio, except Father Byrne in the parish church at Lewisham keeping vigil, watching the Blessed Virgin, who according to rumour stepped through a gap in time, a rent in the suburban stupor. Appearing to her son the priest and simultaneously cancelling someone's bone disease over in the nearby hospital of the Little Company of Mary.

Now, without Father Byrne's knowledge Campbell's agent, a kitchen hand, had begun to speak to the girl of the miracle, the girl whom we had seen at St Martha's in the cardigan with the light dressing on her leg. I still wonder what happened. Was it that she was a country girl scared by the claims being made for her? Did too many people expect her to become a nun? Did she simply want to get away? Did she feel a captive of her own miracle? Or did she just want to see the Big Smoke, Sydney? Campbell's raiders, the kitchen hand told her, could get her out.

According to Mr Frawley's later report, the sort of men Campbell used to infiltrate the kitchens of religious houses were not good solid wowsers like the old-fashioned Rock-ites. They were decadents like Campbell himself. Hence they knew how to talk to simple girls from the bush. She whose osteomyelitis had been remitted was such a simple girl as St Bernadette of Lourdes herself had been. Simplicity can easily be re-directed.

On a Wednesday night in the early winter of 1952, two industrial groupers guarding the convent garden, foot soldiers of the army of light, heard a noise from the hospital's lower floor which was virtually a basement. Campbell's raiders were in. The meat merchant of Homebush who was Mr Frawley's lieutenant was telephoned at once, collected his band of groupers from around Homebush and Strathfield in a matter of minutes and went raging down Parramatta Road towards Lewisham in a series of cars. They ran into a full-blown fist and implement fight with Campbell's rearguard, which consisted of fairly hefty young men stationed by Petersham Cricket Oval to cover the packing of the girl's bag into Campbell's vehicle and her general escape. Stumps and bike chains were used by both sides in that great battle, which saw Campbell's car pull out amidst the mêlée, and then the retreat of the other Campbell forces in the direction of the railway bridge.

Many said that the country girl had shown supreme ingratitude, and avoided her destiny. There would be for her no odour of sanctity, no building of a shrine in her name to which the lame, the blind, the halt would come in darkness and on crutches, and depart upright in light.

This event was yet another example to me of the fact that if you correctly positioned yourself in plain suburban streets, you could be a witness or an actor as absolute good and absolute evil engaged in the earth's most graphic contests. The biggest game in this or any other town. In fact, it was this sort of galactic struggle which in all our minds redeemed Sydney from its distance from everywhere and its then drabness.

Mr Frawley had wielded a cricket stump in that battle and was, therefore, a kind of hero. My father was saved by his World War II-derived cynicism from serving in such a contest, but generally approved of the hard times the groupers had given the raiders. Now witness my father's common man's wisdom in standing aside from the supposed titanic wars of Lewisham and Homebush!

At first the nuns and Father Byrne thought the girl had been abducted and called the police, who within a few days broke the news that the girl had gone off by her own will. Within three weeks, Campbell had her speaking on the platform of the Sydney Town Hall, talking about her imprisonment in the convent. She did not malign Father Byrne, though she told garish stories of the pregnancy of nuns and of unspeakable sins, a term I understood only vaguely but by which I now suppose she meant lesbianism. There were a hall full of bigots and then many more spilling down the steps in George Street. A few groupers in the audience heckled.

Amongst the uninformed, whose thousands packed Campbell's meeting, the sins of nuns and priests were believed to be of such Boccacian frenzy, of such gothic colour. The accusations about child molestation would later sadly be found to have some substance. Certainly nothing was quite as pure as everybody pretended. But the picture was on balance more prosaic. The most common phenomenon would be the chaste and frequently tormented neurotic. And the occasional person who had in full measure that which the system was supposed to deliver more regularly – sanity, joy, hard-won tranquillity. No matter what the sins of priest and religious, they rarely attained the garish form the miraculous girl attributed to them in a packed Town Hall.

For the truth was Brother Basher Bryant consoling himself with a Scotch in the physics laboratory. The truth was the cranky authority of Mother Benignus leading the girls of Santa Sabina in prayer to shield them from the combined concupiscence of St Pat's boys!

When the news about the young woman got out, I think some of us, myself included, imagined encountering this ordinary girl from the country. Talking her around, persuading her back into the care of Father Byrne, back into the shadow of the Little Company of Mary. Something more predictable than that happened: it would eventually become known, and would make the pages of that scandal sheet *Truth*, that Campbell had seduced her, as he did others of his rescued women. She was pregnant with his child. Ultimately, members of that extreme temperance group would lock the doors of *The Rock* to him. But not yet and not that year. That year he would ride high in his hour, a hero on the platform, one who exposed the Papist cant of the convent and the monastery. And when he did fall, it was not his lies which would ultimately be resented by his own people so much as his lecheries. So at least that was universal throughout Christianity – sex was what counted; the main game.

By the very fuss made of it, I knew it was out there, a splendid, glittering, flesh-rending beast, moving in sprung rhythm, wrapped in a mystery which by mid-year, Australia's shortest days in June, I had formed no intention at all of giving up.

And yet to give Father Byrne temporary solace for his other disappointments, I caught the train to Wynyard and walked down to Circular Quay and then boarded the ferry to Manly for a look at life in the major seminary.

An early priest of Sydney, Father Therry, had got the whole of North Head above Manly as a land grant from one of the governors. Manly had been considered remote then, seven miles across the harbour by ferry. By the end of the nineteenth century it had become one of Sydney's chief pleasure and beauty spots. Its long and beautiful surf beach had been a cockpit for the controversy over mixed bathing, and particularly on its sands and on Bondi Beach's further south, the question of what degree of nakedness you could go surfing in was fought out, with an increasing victory going to freedom and flesh. By 1952 beach culture was well entrenched in Sydney, and Manly was one of its loci. But above it all hung on the headland the neo-Gothic magnificence of the seminary, St Patrick's, the architecture a dead ringer for the great seminary of Maynooth in County Kildare, but translated to a sandstone headland in Australia.

The seminary stood behind high sandstone walls and was approached by a long driveway fringed with Norfolk pines. The huge building itself and its appendix of a stone chapel faced northwards, the preferred Sydney direction to catch winter sun. In style, this was one of the few concessions the place made to its Australian location.

As I arrived, a number of boys from several schools were sheepishly collecting in the driveway and being taken in charge by young men in cassocks. These were deacons. Soon they would be ordained. At the end of the year they would go forth as priests and be assigned to parishes. Fresh and dewy, eager and compassionate, they would be adored by parishioners in a way that older, crustier parish priests might not be. Even to someone as young as me, there was something very appealing about their freshness, their new-minted quality. And everyone of them a potential cardinal, a possible first antipodean Pope.

Our group's young deacon introduced himself to us. There were a few St Pat's boys (that is, from the school which bore the same predictable name as the seminary) in our group, but most of the other boys wore the all-blue uniforms which were characteristic of Brothers' schools. The routine was that our deacon, whose name I forget and who would possibly be mixed up and tormented by the great changes ahead in the 60s and 70s, took us first to the chapel. By the chapel entrance was a little glassed-over alcove in which the Cardinal's hat and stole of Australia's first Prince of the Church, Cardinal Moran, were displayed. Moran was something of a hero. He'd supported the strikers in the 1890s, and therefore had a social as well as an ecclesiastical glamour.

Inside, the chapel was wonderful, just like a picture of the medieval monastery. The pews or stalls were very high and faced each other, set up for the singing of the Office. We filed into these unaccustomed stalls and prayed for a short time for guidance on the question of becoming a priest or not. Then the deacon took us through a door by the high altar and we found ourselves in a semi-circular arcade in which a whole series of smaller altars were set in alcoves. The young deacon said, 'After I am ordained in St Mary's, I'll have the honour of saying Mass here at one or other of these each morning.'

Many of these altars were bare of cloths at the moment, and you were able to step up and look at the stone itself, the small slab of engraved marble let into the plainer stone surface, and beneath it a relic of some sort, a fragment of cloth or tissue which had belonged to a prominent saint. For some reason that arcade of altars, that string of divine possibilities, had an impact on me. It is still what I most remember from that first visit.

After the chapel we walked awed into the main building, into the huge stillness of the main corridor, paved like a great chessboard with squares of black slate and white marble. In this broad indoor avenue long as a football field we passed first the rooms set aside to accommodate the professors, then we visited the library, and last the long refectory where the professors and the seminarians ate. During breakfast and the evening meal, someone read from a book chosen by a professor. Sometimes a devotional book, sometimes what the deacon called 'a secular book'. Even books like Paul Brickhill's *The Great Escape*.

We saw a typical room on the upper floors, bed, study desk, cupboard, a few devotional items. The textbooks all in Latin. Glamour to that too. Mangan and I had a taste for the Latin Mass and understood it. The idea of actually studying from books of Philosophy and Moral Theology in Latin was something designed to appeal to a Celestial. It seemed a palpable means of defeating ordinariness and lifting us into a region where we were one with all the other Latin-writing, Latin-speaking clerics and monks of history.

We saw the large Rugby League fields downhill – *mens sana in corpore* etc. The old tag, sane body, sane mind, applied *a fortiori* in a community of celibates.

Also, on the first floor, a museum, and amongst the items a purple set of vestments worn by Blessed Oliver Plunkett, executed under the British Penal Laws. Confessor and martyr.

And another tribute to Ireland – the handball courts on the end of the headland nearest the sea.

At the end, we drank some tea and ate some biscuits in the refectory, on a high table where the rector and the professors ate. Magic again to this. But Sydney University would have its magic and its rituals, too.

We were all awed just the same. A St Pat's boy, Hickey, and myself, in loose formation with other boys in the uniforms of schools we played football against – Marist Brothers Kogarah, Christian Brothers Lewisham, De La Salle Brothers Darlinghurst – walked down Darley Street towards the Manly ferry, chastened. Some of them were promising each other milk shakes at Manly Wharf, as if to console themselves for their brush with a quasi-monastic morning. They felt threatened by the claims of the life they had just looked at, and now they wanted to reassure themselves that 1952 was still in place.

One boy said, however, 'I wanted to join the Redemptorist Fathers, but my mother made me promise not to do it. You don't get seminary holidays at the Redemptorists.'

I had an uncomfortable feeling that the visit to the seminary had put the question to me: how could I be immoral enough to keep stringing Father Byrne along? The prospect was becoming far too real. I dreamed of Blessed Oliver Plunkett's vestments on the first floor at Manly. Freud had not then visited Homebush, and dreams were therefore still prophetic in a way they had been in the Middle Ages. The dream disturbed me because it was unwanted. What I wanted was something which combined the glamour of the priesthood with

the company of either Curran or some other as yet
unimagined helpmeet and hand-holder.

In my mental confusion, I had now found time to write
the essay for the Newman Society competition (winner
and runner-up to be published in the *Catholic Weekly*,
to the acclaim of all relatives). My essay was concerned,
as Dinny had suggested and to no one's surprise, with
the great poems of that lonely Jesuit, GMH: *The Wreck
of the Deutschland, The Windhover, Felix Randal.*

Felix Randal the farrier, O is he dead then? my
  duty all ended,
Who have watched this mould of man, big-boned
  and hardy-handsome
Pining, pining, till time when reason rambled in it
  and some
Fatal four disorders, fleshed there, all contended?

This Jesuit who was the swashbuckler of images, the
Errol Flynn of language.

Towery city and branchy between towers;
Cuckoo-echoing, bell-swarmèd, lark-charmèd,
  rook-racked, river-rounded;
The dapple-eared lily below thee; that country and
  town did
Once encounter in, here coped and poisèd powers ...

My essay was perhaps twenty pages long, and all
in the good handwriting I then had. I had inherited
it from my parents who were both copyplate writers,
given to tall looped Ls and Ps and thoroughgoing Ts
and Fs. When I had the essay done, I walked at nine
o'clock at night to Matt's place and read it to him.
He took the reading with his accustomed tolerance.

I hoped of course that indirectly rumours of my brilliance would get through to Curran. Next I showed it to Dinny McGahan and he was delighted. How many things delighted Dinny! A good slips catch, a good Rugby League sidestep, enthusiasm for a poem.

Waiting for the news of who had won the Newman Society medal, Matt and I spent our Thursday afternoons watching home games of the First XIII. Peter McInnes the great sprinter was on the wing or else in the centres. When he took the ball he sometimes showed instant acceleration. Sometimes, though, he dawdled, teasing the defence into him, perhaps even running infield a little, and then stepping off his infield foot to be gone down the sideline. He had what people like to call *blistering* pace.

I'd spent part of the previous summer running for the Canterbury-Bankstown Amateur Athletic Club with Peter. There had been a desperate ambition in me that Peter's athletic power would somehow enter me through the negligent handshakes we gave each other at the end of races. There was something about the solitariness of sprints and middle distance that appealed to certain souls, the absoluteness of the events. If you failed, you could not hide behind the deficiencies of the group. You knew precisely where you stood in the universe's order. I and everyone else who had been sprinting with Peter since childhood, knew he stood higher than any other boy his age in the Southern Hemisphere if not the universe. The *Daily Mirror* spoke of him as potentially the fastest starter since Jesse Owens, the great black sprinter who had aggrieved Hitler at the Berlin games. Like all great athletes, though, he took talent easily and without assuming airs.

At Belmore Oval, adult athletes predicted greatness for Peter. He ran not against other youths but in the Open Men's, and beat everyone. Our racing uniform for Canterbury was violet with a manure-brown badge. But the colours were only prelude to the colours we cherished – the black, gold, blue of St Pat's.

Going to athletic meetings with Peter each summer Saturday, I found him something of a mystery. He ran for the pure joy. No mug lair. Neither a Celestial nor an oaf. There seemed to be no girl he ran for. If I could have broken ten seconds for the hundred yards as he sometimes did, something other boy-athletes in Australia could not do, I would have laid the bright, blue shell of those broken seconds at Curran's feet.

Sitting with Matt now during the First XIII home games, I watched Peter but was also forced for Matt's sake to pursue another of my avocations – that of sporting commentator. 'It's a St Pat's scrum,' I would tell Matt, 'and Heyes has the ball and gets it out straightaway to O'Connell, who has sliced into the line from fullback and who now draws the Lewisham defence as he gives it to Rowan, and now a lightning pass and McInnes has it, and McInnes has drawn his opposing winger and stepped beautifully inside past him and now has only the tall fullback to beat!'

McInnes nearly always beat the tall fullback and scored.

'Great game, Pete,' Matt would tell McInnes as I steered him over to the champion at the end of the game.

Peter McInnes would thank him in his ego-less manner. 'Good on you for putting your money on us, Matt.'

Sometimes Mr McInnes, Peter's father, would be there and would say to Brother McGahan, 'I just don't want him to pull any muscles before the athletic season.'

That was it: glory awaited Peter and indirectly us as long as a muscle wasn't pulled. Brother Buster Clare had told McInnes that if rounded up in a tackle he was to fall quietly without struggling. No sense a champion trying to hurt himself breaking a tackle when a lot of the time he could evade all the defence anyhow.

A slight chance that he might damage himself stepping from foot to foot was acceptable risk for the prodigy who had come our way and who lived with his parents quietly in Belmore.

Sometimes we would be so inspired by the First XIII's performance that Matt and I would change into running gear after the game and do a few laps with the Nugget tins. Stripped to his shorts and running, Mattie showed he had filled out a lot since last year. Even more than earlier in the year, I could tell by the way he ran that he had the athletic goods. He ran with a brave, high stride. It was just that he needed to run with his head cocked to one side and of course still lost time and direction on the bends. Sometimes I needed to grab him by the elbow, but our aim was to complete the course without having to touch at all, with nothing but sound.

I said to Dinny after one such training session, 'Brother, I think Matt's ready to run against boys of his own age, not just fourteen-year-olds.'

Dinny replied, 'I'd think twice about that, you know. The danger of collision . . .'

In a collision in a race, the orthodox thinking went, a sighted boy could brace himself, but Matt would go into it full force.

I said, 'It would be an important step for Matt.'

'I can understand that,' Dinny conceded. 'We'll see then.'

VI

In the same school, in the shallower levels of that ocean, my brother Johnny, seven years younger than me, went his way and did pretty well from it. He was a natural scholar, accomplished at Maths and a prodigious reader. He had been class captain since third grade, a blond little boy of whom Mrs Banks said that he reminded her of the settlers' flaxen-haired son in *Shane*. He always caught the 414 bus to Homebush station, a sensible kid, no long mooning walks for him. Nor did he ever aspire to carry textbooks of any kind jammed in his breast pocket. In him my father had found an echo of his own nattiness, a consolation for the messy child I had been and still thought it fashionable to be. Sometimes Johnny would miss the bus and I would walk him home, stretching his patience by calling in at the Tierneys' and the Frawleys' for the good sport of posturing and orating. He couldn't see the sense of that, would want to be home attending to his evening in an orderly way, listening to the few radio serials he cherished, doing his impeccable homework. Everybody predicted that he would be a doctor, and they were right. He had fine qualities: stubbornness and a soft heart. He got them both from people like our grandfather the engine driver, and like our grandfather he was temperamentally geared to take a special pride in some profession, in exactitude, in knowing technical matters backwards.

I boasted of him to Mangan and Matt Tierney, and I think he might have taken a certain bemused pride in my eccentric fervours. But our nearly eight-year difference made frontal exchanges between us more awkward than they had earlier been.

It is a truism which people, even memoirists, can't forbear repeating: that to survive childhood is to have memories of non-recurrent chances for filial and fraternal solidarity, for crucial words which went unuttered, for concessions that went unoffered, for gestures which went unsignalled.

Those chances occurred with my father, who was like me in savouring solitariness, working in his vegetable garden in the back yard in Loftus Crescent, but who unlike me had little social life despite his capacity for social charm. It struck me he was mourning for something he couldn't communicate, and something that as a Celestial and an heir to GMH I wasn't interested enough in knowing about. By a happy chance we would both live long enough to become much better friends.

In any case, I was proving to be more of an Australian male than I knew. For I believed as well as he did that male companionship was not for the confession of weaknesses but for the exchange of jokes and bragging. We the sons of the Anzacs and the grandsons of the settlers! Our job to confess to no worries. That fact too stood in the way of a full communion between my father and me. Occasionally we talked of politics and running and Rugby League, and we told jokes, and all that was required to stand for the deeper code of our affection.

Even as McInnes side-stepped and Father Byrne's miraculous girl maligned those who had tended her, two tragedies descended on Strathfield and galvanized our attention.

First: there was a boy who had done the Leaving Certificate the year before and entered the Christian

Brothers' scholasticate, St Enda's, on a plateau behind St Pat's, to study to become a Brother. One night in his dormitory, he developed peritonitis and died within two days. His name was Barnes.

His death as reported to us in class was full of compelling arguments. He had sacrificed a place in the world, had answered his vocation, and met the death he would have met whether he had or not. Just imagine, one of the Brothers said, if he had delayed, if he had not listened to the Call.

All of us were taken out of class and lined Barker Road as Barnes's coffin went by on his way to Rookwood cemetery. He had the holiness of the war dead. He would not get old. He would never lose his freshness, cuff children across the ear in Mathematics class, throw chalk. He had answered the call but not been soured and reduced to ordinariness by it. All that had been required of him were the simple things – to be born, attend St Pat's, answer the call. And his reward would be simple, sublime and eternal. He was to the Brotherhood what Chatterton was to poetry. Eternal because taken too early! I wondered if there had been a Curran in his life, who visited the grave at odd hours. Both Jansenism and Celtic melancholy approved of such an imagining.

Whatever hormonally was happening within me, it was driving me as surely as any biker or hotrodder to the belief that death – to be glorious – should best be consummated in youth. What I would have despised in James Dean, and in the driver of hotted-up Holdens you saw on Parramatta Road, I subscribed to just as actively in my own world view. Barnes's death had its appeal as a way out of the quandary. Better to be a young, slim, untested saint than any plump parish priest or disappointed husband.

That was the first tragedy. Glory interrupted my morbidity over it. A letter came to the school (so that eleven hundred brats could mildly rejoice in the news), announcing I had won second prize in the Newman Society Essay competition. My work was thereby considered good enough to be published in the *Catholic Weekly*.

'Only second prize,' I would say with a hunch of the shoulders to all those who congratulated me. But my mother was delighted in an unqualified way, especially when Dinny told her he had called one of the judges and had been told it was a very close decision. As only an intelligent woman who'd been deprived of it could be, my mother was obsessed above all with her own supposed lack of education. At twelve years she had been allowed to do the Primary Finals in Kempsey, and that was as far as family resources and the times would allow her to go. She had gone to work for ninepence a week, a shop girl at Barsby's Emporium. She served the eccentric bushies who came to town after cloth or buttons, hosiery or corsets.

From this experience she had taken vows that if she had children they were going to go places, and in some ways it was easier to meet her at least halfway than to disappoint her. She had taken intense joy from my first place in the state in English, and had no time at all for my argument that Moose Davitt's manoeuvring with Brother McGahan had contributed to that. It partially confirmed both of us in what could be called our conspiracy of ambition – hers maternal, mine personal. My mother needed little more than this second prize in the Newman essay to confirm that I was a child of destiny. All she innocently asked of life was that her children attain a passable excellence.

The award was to be made in the Newman Society's rooms in Grosvenor Street, Sydney. I knew my mother's enthusiasm and pride might embarrass me and did the sort of thing many an ageing child is later ashamed of – I told her that the event was only for the recipients and the officials of the Newman Society. An obscure amalgam of vanity and lust for independence produced this meanness.

Splendidly solitary in a suit my mother had energetically ironed, I took off for Homebush railway station, three or four hundred yards from home and the scene of all our departures, renewals, and returns from glory and defeat.

On arrival in Grosvenor Street, I was greeted in a panelled room by two youngish men in suits. Very nearly simultaneously with me arrived the first prize winner, an extremely handsome, small, darkish girl of sixteen named Leonie. She had, according to the men in suits, written a killer essay about Christopher Brennan, a tormented Sydney bard, Irish-Catholic, Thomist, alcoholic. It had been a toss-up, one of these officials said, between tormented Brennan and tormented GMH.

Leonie had her parents with her, well-dressed and very proud. She was unabashed by them. Though there was no question of the primacy of Curran, I was excited to find Leonie was both clever and enchanting. Since she was a dazzling child, small as a fourteen-year-old but with a face of mature intelligence, and since I was also clear-eyed and between pimples, it is likely that we looked to Leonie's parents and to the two officials of the Newman Society like the fresh-faced promise of the future.

The Society presented us with a book each. Mine was one I still have – *Elizabethan Recusant Prose*, the writings of the Elizabethans who refused to take their oath to the Queen and remained loyal to Rome. A characteristic Newman Society kind of book, and extremely thick, for the Recusants were enthusiastic pamphleteers ablaze with their rightness, writing in white heat while imprisoned and awaiting the most savage punishments – quartering, the drawing out of their organs while they still lived. Their heroism, too, spread a patina on the night.

I walked back to Wynyard with Leonie and her parents, each of us carrying our massive books and the Society's stamp of approval. There we parted. They were catching a train to the North Shore – somewhere like Pymble. Between us we encompassed Sydney, but hers was the better part. I was never to see Leonie after that night. I wonder what became of her. I can't believe that she trod ordinary paths – I speak not simply out of vanity. Even I could sense her superior latent talent, and find it hard to believe for a second that the result was as close as the officials said.

I kept on telling myself I should visit poor, delivered Barnes's grave at Rookwood and turn there to Hopkinsian verse about it. But things were too busy for me. I had streets to haunt, study time, athletics training, and reading to Matt. And in any case, I was forestalled by the fact that Barnes's incomparable death was superseded in our imaginations by a far more mysterious and utterly tragic one.

It was as if Barnes's perfect, ethereal death had called up an answering one of Satanic and awful nature. A boy from Fifth Year Gold, Buster Clare's class which was so good at Maths and Science, a boy who was repeating the Leaving Certificate in fact in the hopes of a perfect pass and of being awarded the ultimate university prize, an Exhibition, hanged himself in his bedroom in Flemington just a stone's throw from St Pat's.

Flemington, next on the Western Line past Homebush, was of course not a suburb designed for such terrible acts, nor a suburb where people were all at once choked by excessive hope *or* despair.

It was taken for granted by everyone that this was not a deliberate act, any more than Barnes's peritonitis had been chosen. Talking to us about it, Dinny McGahan spoke of the 'balance of the boy's mind'. He had taken his life, but it was certain he was not in theological terms a suicide. His mind could not be guessed at. His torment must have been pitiable.

Since people who were good at Maths and Physics were unlikely to be Celestials, I had not known him except as a fairly restrained presence. He had no particular notoriety and was not a footballer or an athlete of any kind. I had never seen him yelled at or chastized by any Brother. People now said he'd been dissatisfied with his pass the year before in the Leaving Certificate – Second Class Honours in Physics and Mathematics I. The story which was told to explain the unexplainable was that he was a perfectionist who'd gone to pieces in the Physics exam last year and had to be allowed out of the hall at Homebush High – where we sat for the Leaving Certificate – to be sick.

Matt and I and other boys talked about the disaster out on the verandah outside Fifth Year Gold – we'd been advised not to speculate on the event but naturally enough couldn't help ourselves. I heard a boy say, 'He was too bloody scrupulous.' And here we did all begin to edge around the *big* question.

Say he had fallen from grace and continued to go to Communion in that fallen state? An as yet untravelled nightmare country for me, but the young Stephen Dedalus had trodden it and told Honours English boys what is was like in *A Portrait of the Artist as a Young Man*. Had the boy from Fifth Year Gold been there too, and found it unliveable? But to kill yourself, to cut yourself off from mercy. It really wasn't a rational path to follow. All you had to do was to approach cranky, horse-fancying old Father Johnson in Flemington who didn't listen too closely to confessions anyhow. Or the curate at Strathfield who everyone said was so understanding. And so we came back again to the belief that the boy from

Fifth Year Gold couldn't have done it deliberately.

'He was too bloody scrupulous,' was the sentiment everyone returned to. Too much of a perfectionist. He was a lesson on not being too hard on yourself.

Though no one thought he was culpable, only a few prefects were allowed to go to the Requiem Mass, kindly said by Monsignor Loane, which preceded the boy's burial. The school did not line the route to Rookwood as they had for Barnes. As we walked back to St Pat's, strolling informally through the streets of Strathfield as we had never been allowed to in the two-by-two ranks of childhood, one prefect said, 'They reckon he came across his parents *at it*.'

In my chosen Celestial anatomical innocence, I still knew what he meant. The rumour filled the air with nearly too much pain and guilt. I'd seen the devastated mother in the front pew and a portly father, his face unguarded and cruelly pink from grief. And how would they feel, the parents, if what the prefect said was right? So fallen, so degraded, so judged by their boy? And how plausible it all was given the boy's nature, his lust for the perfect. Like Yahweh, finding the world impure, he cursed it. Finding the light sullied, he renounced it. He was the anti-Barnes. No pilgrimages to his sad, sad grave were the subject of daydreams.

We said a rosary for him in class, and then the waters of our remembrance very nearly closed over his head.

The European tradition that women brought dowries to their marriage had gone out of usage in places like Australia, although one occasionally heard the term used in connection with Greek or Italian families. It had not gone out of use to the same extent in the case of girls who went into the convent. By now it had been established that since Rose Frawley was going into the convent she would need a modest dowry to take with her.

Daughters of doctors and lawyers brought superb dowries of thousands of pounds to the convent, and sometimes remembered the Order in their wills. But the Dominican nuns knew – despite the Frawleys' more modest means – the quality of the family and the nature of girl they would have in Rose.

In the Frawley lounge-room, Rose had a highly varnished glory chest placed, just like a girl already engaged to be married, and into it went the specially designed under and outer wear of a novice. Whenever any of us saw it, one or other or us would say, 'You're not *really* going are you, Rose?'

We stereotypically expected the quieter sister to 'go' if anyone went. For the Dominicans were a tough order. They put their novices through a strenuous and penitential course at their novitiate amongst the gum trees at Wahroongah, one of Sydney's quietest northern suburbs. It was hard to imagine companionable Rose tolerating the year's silence the novitiate imposed, and certainly not tolerating unlimited and unquestioning obedience. Chastity, of course, for all of us, seemed the least of problems.

'Fair go,' Rose would say, the idiom of Australia rolling in a mouth which would devote itself to the liturgy and hours of the Office as sung in the thirteenth century. 'Do you think I'd want to stick around just on the off-chance of marrying some joker like you or Mangan?'

Or once she said with unconscious cruelty, 'If Matt was available, I might stick around in the world.'

Matt's snow-white face flushed and we all laughed all the harder to cover her gaffe, her condemnation of Mattie to bachelorhood. And Rose laughed too, the sort of laughter designed to slide discourse along, or to clear its table. She had spoken her most unconscious thought, she had uttered one of the reasons girls from Santa Sabina wouldn't dance with Matt. Without knowing it explicitly, and without any logical reason, they saw Matt as a eunuch for blindness's sake. He could neither be consoled by a beloved nor could he serve the Lord. God had already stricken him. He was exempt both from carnal desire and the need to answer any higher call. Canon Law did not permit the already blind to be ordained. It was possible for men who grew blind after being ordained priests to continue exercising a limited form of priesthood. But if you were blind from birth, neither the dancing girls of Strathfield nor the New South Wales public service nor the departments of the Commonwealth government nor the Holy, Roman and Apostolic Church had a place for you.

Matt took our conversations and all our lapses – Rose's was not unique – with a handsome crooked smile. One wonders if now in middle life the memory of them does not rankle him awake in the middle of the night. For it may not be the primitive slurs of the unknowing and nameless which he most remembers, but our accidental ones, emerging in the midst of friendly talk.

The minimum gear of St Patrick's athletic team members, beside the St Pat's black singlet with its facings of blue and gold, was a black pair of running shorts – in my case sewn up by my mother on her Singer sewing machine – a pair of 'spikes', that is, cutaway black shoes whose soles were arrayed with cruel metal points, and for the very finest athletes, a white sloppy joe. We were not burdened with track suits or starting blocks. I wore my sloppy joe, which my mother could barely afford to buy me, with artistic negligence, the way I wore my school uniform. If it had had a pocket in it,

I would have carried therein some damned book or other.

And our paladin was Peter McInnes. If we went into races doubtful, he was such a certain winner that we could turn up to run on any track in the certainty that he would fill the low points of our performance with his own super-abounding victories. We felt enlarged as runners if he discussed the track surface or spike-length or starting methods with us. We all yearned for that casual stylishness in victory, something which Australian sportsmen from Don Bradman to Ray Lindwall to Clive Churchill possessed. It seemed a mystery to me that you could tell how good a runner was by his manner at the start and the finish. Those of us who were middling tended to force our gestures. Our pre-race warm-ups seemed self-conscious in a way Peter's never were.

The wonderful expectancy, the tension that begs for release, as you shake your limbs out under starter's orders before a race! It is this athletic expectancy which pressed up against the sky, with the chance of anything happening – champions falling, lesser athletes suddenly finding a crucial ounce or two of extra thrust. That throat-swelling, intoxicating stress of the seconds before the start. The casual buzz of the crowd, half-interested in the race but discussing personal things too, the latest Holden car, or some tussle between Dr Evatt and Mr Menzies, all that only spiking up the sense of possibility which the runner feels as the starter, with the right casualness, checks his pistol.

I was aware one late winter Sunday as I stood in a starting lane for an inter-school 440 yards that by the tennis courts, along the back straight, Curran and her two younger sisters sat, having strolled down idly a quarter of a mile from home to watch the meeting.

I knew from the Frawley girls that Curran was a runner also, of greater eminence at the Dominican convent than

I was at St Pat's. She won the 100 yards, the 220 yards
by streets. Running barefooted in a school uniform, as
all the other girls did. Olive legs flashing underneath the
Dominican brown. Convents and even the girls' grammar
schools laid down brown serge cloth against the thighs
of Australia's better women athletes. Only at the club
level, or at the Australian championships, were skimpy,
unimpeding shorts permitted.

Curran could have run at that level, if she had had the
time for it.

On starter's orders, we walked up to our graduated
marks. Ahead of me, in lane four, I could see Gaffney
of St Joseph's College in his pink and lavender, dancing
on the spot and waving and jiggling his hands. I always
wondered why runners jiggled their hands. It implied
that the race brought with it the chance of wrist injuries.
Whatever its purpose, I made sure I did it too.

Down on the mark. We all knew how to take the
posture, few of us knew how to use it to drive away with
the fore and aft leg once the gun went. Peter McInnes
knew. But you couldn't prove your seriousness as an
athlete to people like the Currans unless you could
manage a crouching start. Different matter for the mile,
of course. You could begin the mile with a standing start.
Explosion was not necessary – or even the gesture toward
explosion I was making as I crouched.

I got a good start, at least a fair imitation of an
explosive one. A runner can tell at once, going into
the first bend, whether he is running above himself,
in time with himself, below his best. That day, owing to
some amalgam of physical and psychic causes including
the presence of Curran, I was above myself. I gained two
yards on Gaffney in his outer lane. I knew I had Rankin
beaten, the other St Pat's kid who ate sugary food even
in Lent. Not an ascetic like me. A Celestial. A breeze
from the south-west of the great continent of Australia,

from the interior, swept up and nudged my shoulder as we entered the back straight where Curran and her sister sat. *Give it a go!* it implied. I was Curran's dream athlete envisioned. For her sake I took Gaffney on now with so little effort, shoulder to shoulder. Then out into open air, that lonely space in laned races, that ice-cold, blazing eminence, that kingship under threat. Running in first place, representing Curran, St Pat's and GMH: Keneally.

I could see a little ahead of me the limed lines which marked the start of the 220 yards, and I pounded across my 220 yard line, sensing but as yet ignoring the first aches of breathlessness and muscular failure.

They speak of the wall in the marathon, but the 440 yards or 400 metres has a wall as well, about the 320-yard mark. Those who have been foolish enough by too much flamboyance in the back straight to invite the wall can all at once hear the thunder of their enemies from behind. To the observer it is as if the failing lead runner is being held back by the shoulders. The head goes up or down, a confession of distress, the shoulders begin to waver. In the final bend I could see Gaffney's lavender shirt from the corner of my eye. It went past me like a man-sized spinnaker onto a wind I could not even get a whisper of.

At the turn into the straight, he was five yards ahead and of course uncatchable. This was a good time to perish, to cease upon the hour. Of course, Joey's boys like him were generally boys from the bush. One of our standard primary school essays: *Is it better to live in the Bush or in the City?* Gaffney, the child of some country chemist or solicitor or farmer, was demonstrating the natural superiority of bush cunning and lung capacity.

Cripes, Rankin on my shoulder! Sugar-eater. Girl-fondler. The infrequent visitor to the confessional. The slapdash votary. The fellow who liked Mathematics II better than he liked novels and had never heard of

GMH. He came up in the last half-yard and nudged me by inches.

Dinny McGahan came up and put a hand on my heaving shoulder. 'Young Keneally,' he said, 'ah . . . you had virtually won that race. Just remember next time to save the energy you put out in the back straight, and . . . ah . . . bring it into play at the 320-yard mark.'

Looking at me with one wry eye, he might have understood what led to the back-straight folly. I was in any case humbled by his patience. He must have been certain that anyone who understood sprung rhythm could certainly understand the percentage plan for survival in the 440 yards.

Later in the day, I won the second division 100 yards. Temporary exhilaration. I held myself back in the 220 yards and came second catching up. All this to polite applause. My father, smoking his roll-your-owns in the stand, red-faced from the sun he caught growing tomatoes and Brussels sprouts in the yard, and wearing today his Akubra hat, accepted casual congratulations. This stranger who had come back from wars and to whom I felt responsible. I delayed going to pay filial homage to my parents, since they would remark whimsically on the way I had almost wilfully lost the 440 yards. The results would be inscribed in the *Daily Mirror* as well, which my father bought. Third-placed for eternity in small print under the Port Kembla Race Meeting, the Wentworth Park dogs. The St Joseph–St Patrick's athletics meeting! Could literary critics memorialize a fellow who'd so culpably run third?

I could take only one or two flinching looks to the place where the Currans sat by the tennis courts. They seemed to be talking pretty merrily, as if the world hadn't changed.

I found myself deliberately sampling the despair of that late afternoon to see if it were large enough to explain what the boy from Flemington had done to himself. No, I decided. Not even to take poison like Chatterton, let alone to organize a chair and rope and to decide that the earth had really and eternally lost its elasticity.

Elasticity was the point. I could sense I was too hectically resilient anyhow. And almost at once another chance for a version of excellence came to me like a thrown rope from a kind hand. It required some routine adolescent deceit, but I had already shown at least the normal amount of that. Say I went now and told Brother McGahan or Brother Markwell that my asthma had improved, had behaved better during the winter than anyone expected! I could put myself forward for the nine-stone St Pat's Rugby League team, the team which would be specially put together in August for the State Championships and composed of boys who at the carnival at the Sydney Cricket Ground did not weigh more than 126 pounds. I knew that the team would include a winger called Terry Gale, who was nearly as huge a sprinting prodigy as Peter McInnes. Des McGlynn would captain it, and he had been my captain in the Eight-Stones the year before. He was a very fine half-back. Good man to follow – fresh-complexioned, wiry, brushy-haired, gently tough, and that Catholic sanctifying-grace look in his eyes. His strength is like the strength of two because his heart is pure . . .

This rearrangement of my sporting year would take some good acting on my part. Dinny McGahan had frequently asked me if I was sure the 440 yards was a wise choice, given that I hadn't been able to play Rugby League because of my asthmatic condition. I had quick-wittedly told him that the doctor considered short bursts of energy less dangerous than the continuous, thirty-minutes-each-way effort which Rugby League required. Now this same mythical doctor – it was in imagination Dr Joe Buckley of Homebush, though he'd never actually said these things to me – cleared his grateful patient to play Rugby League again, and anxious to join St Pat's blue, black and gold colours late in the season, I would rush to inform the Brothers.

And as always when we won the State Championship, the Frawley girls would tell Curran, and a small pulse of admiration would emanate from the hill in Strathfield where the Currans dwelt. Democracy would not be offended, I wouldn't be usurping anyone's place, since the nine-stone team was put together for this one series of games spread over two days in the August school holidays. He who was up to scratch got in. On top of that I believed my running training would give me some handy condition.

Before school holidays began, Father Byrne returned to Edgar Street to talk to those boys who had shown an interest in the seminary. He seemed pale with winter paleness and tired with an unrelievable tiredness now. I could imagine some of the worldlier curates saying he ought to play more tennis or golf, and go surfing in the summer. But the world was too much with him already, and was not the cure for him.

I went to the parlour in the Brothers' house to meet him and he told me, 'The Cardinal and the rectors of the two seminaries intend to interview boys interested in studying for the priesthood. The interviews are to be held at the Presbytery of St Mary's Cathedral on the first Saturday of the August holidays.'

That would be the day after the Nine-Stoners won the State Championship. For who could oppose us?

'Six other boys from the Leaving Certificate class intend to go for the interviews,' said Father Byrne. 'This does not necessarily commit the boy who is interviewed to becoming a seminarian. Indeed, many fail the interview due either to lack of intelligence or obvious lack of virtue. I would be happy to arrange for you to attend the interviews if you wish. I believe you have the right qualities.'

Even though the thought of it filled me with an electric and not utterly pleasant sense of expectation and unreality, and on top of that made me sweat, I agreed to enrol myself for such an interview for fear of disappointing him further, of deepening the dark night he was obviously experiencing. But how do you talk to a Cardinal, or more specifically to Cardinal Gilroy? And to the rectors? Poor Father Byrne would have to be disappointed in the end, but there was time for that.

But even now I wondered what device I could use to extricate myself in the end. I had already earmarked for other purposes the stratagem of fictional advice from a doctor. I could hardly make up fictional advice from an invented father-confessor who would tell me I was unfit in his opinion to be a seminarian and so would get me off the hook.

Some ruse which didn't actually offend the heavens would present itself though, I was sure. In the meantime, there was the glimmer of vanity Father Byrne in his innocence held out: to prove yourself intellectually and morally fit. You would come out knowing you were up to scratch for the seminary and that a Cardinal knew it too.

'I'm not utterly certain, father,' I told the priest under a photograph of priests who'd done their schooling at St Pat's. 'But I think I'm close enough to justify going for the interview.'

'So do I,' said Father Byrne. He had believed the miraculously cured renegade, who now appeared on Campbell's platforms to denounce Papist perfidy. Why shouldn't he believe a sly little bugger like me?

I left in fear. The sweet, glamorous state of quandary with which I indulged myself would end. This was late July. Uncertainty, the glimmering surface of a thousand opportunities, was a winter delight, and I saw now however vaguely that the axe of exams and definite choice would fall in the late spring and early summer. Then all dilettantes and pretenders would be shown up. I was not of constant stuff like Mangan, who was directed with gleaming certainty towards that little slice of the thirteenth century which lay in the hills outside Melbourne.

Brother Markwell held the trials for the nine-stone team about ten days before the August holidays began. Many of us had played together in earlier teams though. We knew each others' moves. I felt again that miraculous primeval sense of the inflated bladder landing squarely in my arms. Markwell was a great driller of Rugby League players. We never looked at the tackler however menacing he might be. We looked only at the chest of the man we were throwing the ball to. If defending, we watched the attacker's hips and applied our shoulders to the hams while our arms grasped across the knees, pushing with our shoulder, creating an irresistible system of fulcrumage which brought them all tumbling down – Marist Brothers Kogarah, James Cook High School, Cleveland Street, Marist Brothers Darlinghurst, Fort Street, Christian Brothers Lewisham, Parramatta High, Patrician Brothers Ryde.

I had done such a perfect tackle on Brother Markwell himself the year before, when he decided to take part in a limited game with us. As he fell I'd freakishly broken my nose against his hipbone, but the reward was he knew what I was capable of.

Just the same, I did find I was short of a run now. As footballers said, jogging was no substitute for match fitness, the sort of fitness that came from tackling and

being tackled, from finding your place in the back line
or the forwards after each passage of play.

Besides, I was anxious about telling my parents about
the interview with the Cardinal. I knew it would not be
entirely welcome news. I had passed off my earlier visit
to the seminary as curiosity. It was impossible to try the
same excuse to cover an interview with a Cardinal.

I went first to my mother, the intermediary between
my father and myself. She interpreted the one to the
other. I told her in the little dining-kitchenette which
had been our hearth in the fraught, close years of my
father's absence. As soon as I had the words out I saw
genuine terror cross her face.

I said lightly, 'It doesn't mean anything. I'll probably
go to uni, but if I wanted to be a priest I think I'd
rather go to one of the Orders.'

She knew that the Orders meant that she wouldn't see
me for years, the child she had nursed and urged back
to breathe and coaxed to some scholarly eminence, and
she broke into tears. I was of course of an age where
everything is easily sacrificed – family, love, even life.

'You must promise me you won't go into the Orders,'
she said.

Even I was moved by the authority of her fear. Perhaps
too I had an over-inflated view of my capacity to talk her
around later, if it came to that.

'Your father will be very disappointed, poor fellow,'
she told me. 'What should I tell him?'

I thought that perhaps and for once I should approach him, though with our mutual embarrassment
towards each other, I wondered how successful that
telling would be. From the back screen door I was
happy to watch her breaking the news to him. As he
stood in his little garden at the back of the yard we
shared with the Bankses. Mrs Banks would watch from
behind her own screen door and later report a mixed-up

version of what she had witnessed to her husband and her daughter.

It was not the best of years for my father. He was not entirely happy with work – he had fights with my aunt and uncle-in-law in whose store in the Western Suburbs he worked. He did not know where to go. But his sons would go somewhere, he was certain. The seminary was amongst the last choices he would want. I would find out later how tribal a man he was, how he would cherish and be exalted and validated by grandchildren.

In the end, I didn't do the telling of my father myself. But I did give my mother some advice. Above all, I wanted her to stress that this interview did not mean I would go to the seminary. That was certainly the case. If I had been honest enough I could have come clean and said, 'I'm going only to keep Father Byrne happy.' But I was ashamed to admit it.

Watching from the back door as my mother broke the news, I saw my father pause, lean on his pitchfork and look away to the vivid winter sunset over Granville. But I knew my mother was bringing him around, taking my intentions more seriously than ever they deserved to be taken.

※※※※※

Back on the train that late August, on the ochre beast which ran beyond my parents' front windows. We Nine-Stoners got aboard at Flemington, Homebush, Strathfield, Burwood. We carried our football boots and socks and padded shorts in the same bags in which we at other times carried our schoolbooks. Globite bags which had their own smell of banana skins and Mathematics and History.

At Central we carried them aboard the special buses laid on for the carnival to take hordes of suburban and bush footballers to the Sportsground-Cricket Ground area of Moore Park. Aboard the buses a piquant excitement grew, and moves and sprigs and the desirability of shoulder pads were discussed as we neared the holy grounds of Rugby League. We changed in the freezing dressing sheds at the Sportsground or Sydney Cricket Ground II, and found ourselves being pointed out for our black and gold and blue jerseys, which I am still proud to say meant a threat to all the players from other places and schools.

Brother Markwell handed out resin for rubbing on our hands. In case we forgot the fundamental rules of passing and catching it would help the ball to stick. Although we knew no amount of resin could save a player who tried to take the ball with his finger tips.

It took two and a half days to win the State Championship, and Brother Markwell played me in four games and two half-games (that is, bringing me on at half-time, or taking me off then). On Sydney Cricket Ground II, we bowled over the first couple of schools we faced. Our mode was casual efficiency. We were proving what the Brothers had told us, that the state schools didn't have a chance, their coaches were not a celibate élite. Their coaches in fact had children to go home to, and so their attention was divided. We got the ball out to Ballesty, whose brother would play Rugby for Australia, and to Gale, who would represent Australia in the sprints at the Commonwealth Games. And they would go roaring down the flank, since we would already efficiently have drawn all the defence to us.

The semi-final was played against Lewisham on the Sydney Cricket Ground itself, the holiest turf. Bradman and Tiger O'Reilly had worked here against the England XI, and the Rugby League Messiah Clive Churchill had his great kicking duels with the immortal French fullback Puig-Aubert. I was only a reserve for the Cricket Ground game – I ran on for seven minutes at the end.

Brother Markwell told me he was saving me for the final against Marist Brothers Eastwood. And what did it matter anyhow, as long as we won the final and the rumour of it all got back to Santa Sabina and to Curran?

The Frawley boys, Rose's and Denise's little brothers, were at the Sydney Cricket Ground watching from the sideline. So the lines of intelligence were in place, since they were sure to take the news back to their sisters, who would then become crucial broadcasters of it.

The final was played in late light on Sydney Cricket Ground II, before a sizeable crowd of boys in the uniforms of various schools. The opposition's coach had given them a scheme by which they could choke off the ball in the hands of our inside backs or mobile forwards. They were all over us. Their desperation showed they understood that the ball couldn't be allowed to get to Gale or to Ballesty. It became a grudging, hard-tackling game. Bobby Maloney, whose first two names were Robert Emmet in honour of the great Irish nationalist of 1803, crashed over for a try. But then Eastwood struck back. Five-all. Ballesty kicked a goal, and then they kicked a goal, seven-all. Naturally, this was the sort of triumph which on reaching the cloisters of Santa Sabina would fail to cause much of a sense of excitement.

I remember taking the ball up the middle of the field, determined to break the net of tacklers, never able to do it. For grace had gone out of all of us. We had become the day labourers of the game. We squabbled with Eastwood for the ball in a muddy corner of the field. We were like Matt Tierney's father's army before Ypres. Bogged down. It was seven-all at full-time, but the game belonged to us on countback – we had scored the first try. We were state champions by a technicality.

The concept had a faint glow, which I became accustomed to while travelling home on the train from

Central Railway with the Frawley boys. Again, obvious glory had side-stepped me, or me it, for I had played my lungs out. Will was not enough and grace was everything. Peter McInnes had grace. The nine-stone team, at the supreme hour, had not been given it.

It was dark already when I got home to my parents and little brother, doing my best to sound excited at having become a State Champion by a technicality. But I knew that now, overnight, it was a matter of preparing for the other contest, the grievous sport: to be declared fit for a priesthood I had no intention of entering. I was aware that such nets of vanity held me, yet I had thought I was free. What was I doing, wasting a Cardinal's time? I could not really envisage myself a seminarian. I thought of the priesthood the way I thought of death in battle – an admirable but unimaginable destiny.

And so, anxious and pallid, I was back by nine o'clock onto Sydney's rust-red electric trains. The river of our lives, carrying such freight – my grandparents arriving from Kempsey, my father returning from wars, myself returning from second place essay prizes or technically-won State Championships.

This morning I brought a not unpleasant post-match soreness to the terrifying cosmic business of being declared, by a Cardinal, an Eminence, a man who'd spoken to the Pope, fit for the corps. I was so worried by the coming meeting that I levered my copy of GMH out of my pocket and after trying to smooth down my suit, left it behind.

Off at Town Hall station and walk up Park Street, through Hyde Park, a parade ground in the days when Australia was a British colony. Now marked in the middle by the nationalistic fountain of Archibald, the founder of the nineteenth-century journal the *Bulletin*. Tired mothers sat on the edge of the fountain as children ran and fell and dipped their hands in water. They were like foreign populations seen from a train window. For these few hours I would belong to a different world from theirs. I am ashamed to say that I despised the plainness of them, the plainness of Menzies' Australians.

Ahead the great Gothic mass of St Mary's. It lacked spires, for they had been planned to go atop the western end of the nave, but the archbishops of Sydney had always lacked the means to do them. If delivered from this ordeal, I could imagine myself as a good Catholic layman, wealthy from some unspecified cause, perhaps from writing G. K. Chesterton-like books or GMH-like poetry, endowing the cathedral so that a spire could be raised. An umbilicus connecting Sydney to the sky and to the Gothic tradition Mangan and I so loved.

I rounded the flank of the cathedral and followed up sandstone steps a sign that said *Minor Seminary Interviews*. A stone doorway austere as a vow carried a similar sign. I could hear subdued conversation inside. I stepped indoors.

I would later find out from travels elsewhere in the world that the severe decorousness of convent and presbytery architecture is universal. Sombre wood panelling, bare walls except for a photograph of St Peter's or the Pope or both, and on a stand in a corner the Virgin crushing the serpent with her foot. The floors in turn are bare but highly-polished, and the cold smell of the beeswax which brought them to such a high shine pervades. There is none of the hutch-like aroma that exudes from homes where real, squabbling families live. There is instead a cold clarity of air. The atmosphere had been imported from places like Dublin and Maynooth. From this clarity, arctic even in the climate of Australia, it seemed only a short and elegant shuffle to the eternal clarity.

I think all the boys from ordinary hutch-like places, Homebush or Darlinghurst, Kogarah or Belmore, felt the magnetic pull of that air. As I entered the waiting room, I noticed how this atmosphere made their Celtic flesh paler, brought out their freckles. My fellow interviewees wore the uniforms of sundry Marist and Christian Brothers schools. I wasn't sociologically imaginative enough then to realize that most of them came from the same sort of schools which produce the New South Wales Police Force – hardly anyone from the North Shore, or from the Jesuit colleges which played Rugby instead of Rugby League or put boat crews in the Head of the River. I saw not demographics but only the chosen-ness of this group. For the first time, I felt an impulse genuinely to belong amongst them. In military situations, I suppose, this is called *esprit de corps*, and all armies depend on it, even the armies of the Lord.

I was, however, not unconscious of the fact that amongst this group St Pat's was something of an aristocracy. We wore grey serge rather than blue, our felt hats were sported with the cockiness of great Rugby League players, and we now had all the casually acquired State Championships we needed to prove it.

I saw that John Hickey was there, a tall boy from St Pat's who didn't know whether he wanted to be a lawyer or a priest. I sat beside him. His dark hair had been lustrously brilliantined.

'I don't know if I want to be in this place,' he murmured to me. 'I think I might like women too much.'

'I feel exactly the same thing,' I told him. I patted the empty space where GMH had lain inadequately exploited over my right breast. That pocket which was somehow associated in my mind with love.

'Can you really concentrate when they're around?' he whispered.

I remembered the fatal quarter-mile race I'd lost through lack of concentration. I said, 'Just because we're thinking of the seminary, it doesn't mean we're obligated to anything.'

Yet I could feel the atmosphere of obligation working on me. I knew in my water that once I got in there with the Cardinal and the rectors, I mightn't be able to stop myself saying something which was halfway to being a promise. Too much magic, too much authority to resist.

Hickey picked up a book from the floor. It was Windeyer's *History of Australian Law.*

'What have you got that for?' I asked him.

'Cripes,' he said, shaking his head. 'I thought I'd take it in with me to let them know I'm not certain.'

I all at once wished I had brought GMH for a similar reason – both to protect me and strengthen me. Yesterday Hickey had played reserve when the First XIII had won the State Championship. He hadn't needed any protection out there. This was, however, of course, a serious battlefield.

'These other blokes here feel the same way,' Hickey confided in me, and I checked again the pale faces. I tried to see the future bishops behind the freckles and the acne.

We went over the top one at a time. In the presence of the Pope on the wall, the jokes that were uttered as each boy went out were in a lowered voice and accompanied by what you would have to call graveyard humour. 'Don't forget to tell them about that girl from Saint Scholastica's.' No reference to masturbation. These were not those kinds of boys. No reference to homosexuality, which was an unimagined and unimaginable kingdom of night, at least as yet, to everyone in the room.

The Ahernes, the Clancys, the Doughertys, the Fitzgeralds went in alphabetical order of their first names, and when Hickey was called by a young priest who waited in the corridor with a list, the gravity of the event became more intense still. I noticed though that Hickey had not found the courage to take in his law book. It stood by the leg of his chair, an abandoned love.

A couple of Kellys from sundry suburbs stood between

me and the enquiries of the Cardinal. Cardinal Gilroy's voice, the one all schoolboys occasionally made fun of. It seemed to have been a voice devised in the Collegio di Propaganda Fidei in Rome, where the stars of the seminary were to finish their studies. It was designed more for speaking ecclesiastical Latin than English, and it penetrated the soul. It could not be imagined what it was like to face it as a solitary listener in an august room.

The Kellys now went in one at a time to the Cardinal and came out pale, making for the street and the secular world, relieved of a burden. Determined either to go or not to go. To become a seminarian or put it off until the meeting with that sensual, secular girl who would render the choice irrelevant.

My name was called. Walking forward in unreal space, in the hushed but heel-clacking corridor, I knocked on the indicated door and heard the extraordinary voice. 'Come in, my young man.'

I entered. There he was, the Cardinal in black and scarlet, sitting tall behind a long mirror-shined table.

'Please sit down.'

I felt very small crossing the polished boards to him and the other ecclesiastical presences. Scarlet cardinalatial piping connected the sections of His Eminence's soutane, and the broad scarlet sash sat high, just under his sternum. The Cardinal and the two men who sat either side of him wore birettas, or priests' hats.

'Hello Your Eminence,' I said, so they wouldn't think me a bumpkin.

And then His Eminence indicated his partners, on his left, Monsignor Cary of St Columba's Minor Seminary at Springwood in the Blue Mountains. Monsignor Cary was built heftily, like a cop or a publican. Then on the Cardinal's right, Monsignor Mahony, rector of the great St Patrick's College Manly.

'I have been remarking to the other boys,' the Cardinal

told me after I settled in the chair in which it was impossible to sit with ease, 'that it is a little like surviving in a holy war. Getting from Monsignor Cary's to Monsignor Mahony's seminary. The inevitable losses account for perhaps three in ten young men. And yet the process is necessary and ordained by the Church's long experience in ecclesiastical education. It is much better that a young man lose a few years testing his vocation in the minor seminary than that he should go out into the world and lose his vocation there on the streets, or amongst so-called intellectuals.'

They all three looked at me, the Cardinal and Mahony smiling, Cary seeming to suspect me of breaking and entering.

'That is my concern, Your Eminence,' I managed to tell Cardinal Gilroy. For, as a natural competitor, I did not want to be seen to be passive but to be a fellow capable of word-making in any situation. Just the same, I judged from the look of suspicion on Monsignor Cary's big meaty face that he saw right through me.

The Cardinal looked at the dossier from St Pat's.

'I see you are studying Leaving Certificate Latin and attempting Honours History and English.'

'That's right, Your Eminence.'

'And placed second in the Newman Essay Prize.'

'Yes, Your Eminence.'

'Very promising,' said Monsignor Mahony, who looked like Pius XII, a wiry little man whose false teeth fitted him badly and slewed around his mouth. He was by temperament jovial however, unlike his colleague.

'Students who are good at English are very frequently capable of great vanity,' said Monsignor Dunne. 'I suppose you're vain like the rest of them?'

'I hope not, Monsignor,' I lied. 'My hero is Gerard Manley Hopkins, who was both a great poet and a man who fought vanity.'

'Don't know him,' said Monsignor Cary.

'He was the Jesuit priest who asked on his death bed that his poems should be destroyed.'

'Probably a good idea,' said Monsignor Cary.

'And you play Rugby League, I notice,' said His Eminence, breaking up the impasse.

Monsignor Mahony said, 'It's the day of the year when the St Patrick's Manly team play the St Columba's Springwood team.'

His unfortunate teeth clacked with his honest enthusiasm.

The Cardinal came in with the big question. 'Have you made a definite decision yet, my dear young man?'

The skewering question which all but the most certain dreaded. If I told him yes, could Curran be depended upon to weep at once? Or would she laugh like a drain, like the Frawley girls?

'I feel the ultimate decision is very, very close, Your Eminence.'

Monsignor Cary's omniscient eye made me feel that it had better be, that I'd better stop wasting his time.

The Cardinal said, 'You must pray to Our Blessed Mother, the mother of us all, for the guidance you need. You are a communicant four or five days a week according to your file. That is a sign of your seriousness, and in the seminary, you will have the leisure to be a daily communicant. It may be in fact what you are intended to be. And imagine what it would be to achieve the ultimate stature of being a priest of God, transforming through your words the substance of bread and wine into the body and blood of Our Lord Jesus Christ. To think that you, a young man from Homebush, should be given that divine and eternal privilege!'

There was nothing to be said in reply. I smelled the incense, I recited in my head the sonorous Latin. I intoned the *Gloria in excelsis Deo*. This ritual the one item of grandeur in crass old Sydney. I felt surge in me the power of sacramental rites: the rite of the confessional, the rite of Extreme Unction – Last Anointing. GMH had written of giving it to Felix Randal the farrier.

> Sickness broke him. Impatient he cursed at first,
>   but mended
> Being anointed and all; though a heavenlier heart
>   began some
> Months earlier, since I had our sweet reprieve and
>   ransom
> Tendered to him . . .

I felt for a second the divine intoxication of GMH's words, the transcendent value of these mercies. Then the enchantment broke and was succeeded by a freezing terror. They almost had me! All I could do was say that I expected a decision soon. I looked once more and flinchingly at Monsignor Cary's large, rather droopy eyes. He knew I was a chancer. A dilettante.

'It was very pleasant meeting you, young Mr Keneally,' said the Cardinal. Prince of the Church. Again I remembered that according to the *Mirror*, Cardinal Gilroy might become the new Supreme Pontiff, infallible when speaking *ex cathedra* on matters of faith and morals. I was trying to play ducks and drakes with him. I was using him as lever to the acquisition – whatever that acquisition entailed – of beautiful Curran.

'It might prove,' I found myself ridiculously telling the two monsignors and the Cardinal before I left, 'that this meeting has been the crucial one.'

When I left it was with that same sense of escape as I had seen on the faces of the others. Into beautiful Macquarie Street. Amongst Menzies' beautiful, secular, un-knowing people. Past the old convict barracks, the Registrar-General's department where honest Protestants worked without claims to infallible authority. The Archibald Fountain spraying its secular, humanist water.

I felt seamless joy. But I feared a return of the divine exaltation I had experienced in the Cardinal's presence.

VII

Soon a letter came from the Cardinal's secretary asking me to let the authorities know by the end of November what my decision was, so that a place could be set aside in Springwood seminary. Naturally I showed it to my mother, more from the point of view of being found suitable than as someone definitely going to the place. My mother took the normal mother's pride in the idea that a Prince of the Catholic Church found her son adequate. She went and showed it to my refugee of a father, estranged by the aloofness of his smart-alec son.

At least he still had my brother, who talked without restraint with him. And as a carpenter *manqué*, he still made things for Johnny. He knew that these gifts would in Johnny's case not be dismissed as inferior to the works of GMH. He made Johnny pencil boxes and small cases for things. He ran them up on the balcony as the trains went by, and then lovingly lacquered them. Amongst Australian males, the coat of lacquer was one of the permitted expressions of affection.

He had once made me too a lacquered schoolbag of wood, metal clips in every corner, and an accurately fitted lock. It had done me three years until one day in 1950 I carelessly left it in the shallow gutter. While I was discussing Brother Markwell's Latin class with Mangan, the 414 bus backed over it and reduced it to splinters and tyre-marked textbooks. That – though not intended by me – was like the close of childhood.

Now my mother showed the Cardinal's letter to my father. As usual I did not show it to him myself.

Afterwards though, I presented it in person to the Frawley girls and the Tierneys. None of them were more than moderate spreaders of news. But the word got around that way.

I received some discouragement. Crespi the salesman stopped me one morning in Homebush Road.

'Do you know,' he asked me, 'that in the Spanish Civil War the Republican forces shot priests? These were decent armed young fellows, and they shot priests. Why do you think so? Not because they hated the Church in itself. No. Because the priests were enemies and exploiters of the people. Ordinary people knew. If you became a priest, you became an oppressor of minds and bodies.'

It was nothing I did not expect to hear, and I was not disturbed.

When we rested during training for the athletics carnival, Matt would ask, his head held sideways, 'Have you made up your mind yet, Mick?' Even then I think he gauged all of us accurately and forgave us our vanities.

'I don't believe it's for me,' I told him, though the immaculate and arctic atmosphere of the Cathedral house still remained with me and I fell asleep savouring it.

In the meantime I was all studied indecision. To endure in divine uncertainty, stuck between the cloister and the hearth made me – I was sure – a figure of great dramatic interest. I believed I would get away with it too. That awesome sense of the priesthood as seen from the inside by GMH and the Cardinal had not recurred to me.

Only the wise saw me more as a rabbit caught between headlights.

Indeed the further I got from the interview with His Eminence the more middling cosy and ordinary the life of the diocesan seminary seemed to be. For one thing, you came home every year. Those who went to the Franciscans or the Passionist monastery (called the Passionate Fathers by the ignorant and the mocking) did not come home to be fed up by their mothers during Christmas vacations. They did not become priests who played golf. They lived as if golf had not been invented.

I knew now in an academic sense that my mother and father would give their reluctant consent to my going into the seminary, if I decided on that. Because no one could stand in the way of the divine intent. My mother had already touchingly begun to observe, with those research capacities which mothers have, the relationship between young curates around Sydney and their mothers. She had spoken to a Mrs Aherne at Flemington whose son was a priest. Mrs Aherne was very pleased with her lot. She told my mother that in the world, boys marry and often did not have time for their mothers. But for a priest, the mother remained the chief relationship. The son, the priest, could devote a lot of his time to his mother and be a true filial companion.

This had consoled my mother somewhat. But having come like my father from a tribal family, she was no more than consoled. She would have liked the prospect of grandchildren, a prospect which seemed to me remoter than becoming the conductor of the Berlin Philharmonic.

My father would come in and say sometimes, gloomily but without aggression, 'Why don't you get a degree first in case it doesn't work out?'

But Father Byrne had prepared me to deal with such proposals.

⊗⊗⊗⊗⊗

Meanwhile, Brother Digger Crichton, who had seen the Red Baron fall, would sometimes say at large assemblies on the last Friday of September, 'Every boy has his last Sports Day.'

It was a plain enough statement with its intimations

of mortality and change and decision. It bore down strenuously on me. Soon I would have to come clean on the seminary. Soon I would have to step back into ordinariness and decide on university.

Matt and I were prepared for the Sports. Matt ran in bare, strong, snow-white feet. His upper legs were even better developed from all our training, the hairs on his body utterly white. His mother's German measles, which had made him a snow baby in the womb, had penetrated even to the follicles.

He and I were members of the team called the Reds – in anti-Communist Australia, the colour still had an innocence when applied to running teams. Terry Heys, a future academic, was captain of the Reds, and I was vice-captain. Brother Basher Bryant, the Brother in charge of the Reds, obviously mercifully felt he could not deny the intensity of my desire to be identified as an athlete.

I approached him after our team meeting to discuss what race against other sixteen-year-olds Matt would run in. He showed me he had slated Matt for the fifth heat of the Under 14s.

'But we've been training,' I protested, barely able to hide my anger. 'Just so that Matt can run against people his own age.'

'Yes,' said Basher Bryant definitively. 'But he isn't very certain in the way he runs and I don't want any collisions.'

'He'll be very disappointed,' I told Basher.

'Are you arguing with me?' he asked.

'It's not fair to him. He could beat people like Mangan.'

'I expect a more cooperative and obedient attitude,' said Basher.

'Yes, well, if you'd told us earlier we could have saved ourselves a lot of training.'

'That's enough of that,' said Basher.

I saw that the thing to do was to appeal to Dinny. But before I could do that, I had to go down the room and fetch Matt. My rage was such that I couldn't keep the news in. As I spoke to him, Matt remained preternaturally still.

'I'm going to get Dinny to fix it up for us,' I told him.

'Don't, Mick,' he said.

'No, Dinny won't stand for it.'

But his face reddened in that astounding way and his enunciation was taut with fury. *'Don't!'* he told me. He was so authoritative at such moments.

'But we've trained so hard,' I told him.

Matt, however, was determined to get even with Basher by accepting the limits others put on him. I said we should both refuse to compete, but at St Pat's that was like refusing to breathe.

Matt looked away into darkness, and as much as I pleaded would not let me take our case to Dinny.

It was in fact so compulsory to participate in Sports Day that Mangan the future Trappist was there shamelessly bare-footed, for running shoes were beneath his dignity.

'Oh, my heaven,' he told me. 'I feel so vulgar in primary colours.'

Lanky Larkin, the apprentice agnostic who these days spent only a little time amongst the Celestials, was in a blue singlet for the last time in his life, suffering this last indignity of his boyhood. He had begun to meet up with Sydney University Philosophy students at pubs in Forest Lodge, and the secular heresies sang to him as he stood slightly goose-fleshed and self-parodied in the vest of the Blues.

A photographer from the *Mirror* had come to take a picture of Matt and me crouching in our lanes, and we did not bother informing him of Basher's cruel edict. Early arriving parents sportingly applauded Matt as he took up his crouch. Then a group picture – Terry Heys, Matt, myself, Peter O'Gallagher the 880-yards runner.

'What about you, Curly?' the photographer called to Mangan in an attempt to make a crowded photograph.

'I'm a sporting leper,' Mangan cried to him, but joined in, Byronic martyr to Australian sporting philistinism.

Whenever the Reds won a race, Heys and I and other gun athletes were meant to run in front of the team on the benches by the dressing rooms called the Stockade and lead the rest of the Reds in their war cry.

> Eero, eero, eero rum,
> Rum stick a bopple
> On a zip man golliwoggle,
> Down with Green, Gold, Blue . . .

For me this was a half-sweet day, since I knew I would not excel adequately in any one event to make it into the supreme team, the team which ran against the other colleges on the Sydney Cricket Ground. And then the closed subject of the race Matt had to run in.

I was third in the shot-putt in the morning, against a background of little boys running their hearts out.

'Eero, eero, eero rum . . .'

My little brother, a blond-haired member of the Greens, had never been a runner. I stood in my representative's singlet of black and gold and blue, yelling him on in his age group. He had never been well-coordinated except in the academic sphere, where he was dazzling. But unlike Mangan he did not despise athletics or athletes, though he had a sensible unwillingness to flay himself. Equal quantities of vanity and desire had won me my black singlet. My little brother was content with his green. And though he didn't particularly like me coaching him in races, I thought it a fraternal duty to do so.

As for the serious stuff, I won the *Second* Division

100 yards and was overtaken by one other boy in the 220. Peter McInnes, the wonder of the meeting, whose picture had been taken solo by the *Mirror* photographer earlier, steamed down the grass to win his age race (he was some months younger than the rest of us) in 9.9 seconds. A standing ovation, which he took with a very small ration of smile.

Matt ran with apparent full force against fourteen-year-olds in the 220 yards. He did better at the bends than at the 100 yards, in which he still ran uncertainly, baulking sometimes, down the stretch of the field. Perhaps Basher had been right or perhaps Matt – though he didn't seem to be – was dispirited. In any case, he ran third. But in the 220 yards, following the rattle of the Braille type in the shoe polish tins, he ran with enough certainty to win. I laconically shook Matt's hand and uttered my *Goodonyers*. He got the only standing ovation of the day other than the one for Peter McInnes, and waited beside me with his head half cocked, his chin enquiringly lifted until the crowd had stopped clapping. As his parents did, he secretly wondered whether the applause was not outright pity.

In that way, on that bright September Saturday, Matt and I stood in the sun imitating true athletes.

I cannot even remember which team won that day. *Eero, eero, eero rum* or one of the other three. The march-past remains as a composite memory from my eight years of marching past my parents as a St Pat's child. We all lined up in fours behind our flag and Brother Crichton played a record or *The Stars and Stripes Forever* by Souza, the same marching tune on the same record, which he'd been playing since I was eight years old.

At the end of the afternoon, the mile was run. The world was full of talk of the four-minute mile that year. There were actually small boys who thought, What if I break that barrier today? That was the improbable lure.

Red-headed Pog O'Gallagher and a small ferrety boy called Simon were the best milers, and Simon had run four minutes thirteen seconds. Thirteen seconds did not seem to us in our innocence much of a barrier. Matt and I even started the mile, as did my little brother in his green singlet. After our efforts of the day, I knew we would not be expected to run more than a lap, and so loping along, my hand on Mattie's elbow, we bade our farewell to St Pat's athletic tradition.

My little brother Johnny, having dashed away into the mile like a ferret, was flagging after a lap and a half. I called, 'Come on, Johnny.' Just a *pro forma* cry. I was horrified to see the exhausted boy turn back onto the track and continue for another asphyxiating three hundred yards. I found myself half-ashamed at the fraternal power I had discovered myself to have.

We waited until Monday afternoon to see the picture of ourselves and Matt on the *Mirror*'s back page.

Inside the back page lay a more serious, hard-hitting article on Peter McInnes. John Treloar, the Olympic sprinter, said Peter had now beyond all remaining doubt confirmed himself as Australia's greatest sprinting prospect. Yet Peter was in class on Monday morning with his Maths homework done. All that splendour concentrated in him.

He made me feel the un-holiness of being a pretend athlete, a pretend seminarian. The duty of breaking the news to priests and cardinals would soon descend.

✧✧✧✧✧

Now there was hardly anything between us and the season of frantic study. In six weeks we would begin going to Homebush High to do our public examinations, the very examinations whose prospect had – according to conventional wisdom – killed with a noose the boy from

Flemington. In a week or two we would be issued our exam numbers, which we would put instead of names on all our answers. I was beginning to come to grips with more T. S. Eliot and Auden than I had earlier in the year and even with some Shelley and Keats as well. But I had taken a vow that it would be a good Honours English exam question that would prevent me writing about GMH. For the Honours History exam I was up on all the totalitarian systems.

At the inter-school competition at Sydney Cricket Ground, running on turf which in the winter was used as a Rugby League pitch and which in summer was the outfield for Cricket Test Matches, Peter blistered down the 100 yards in 9.8. I was a mere reserve for the 100 metres relay, which meant that I had to sit in the stands with Matt, contented enough and leading the war cry.

> Black, black, rickety-rack,
> S P C is on the track . . .

There was plenty of opportunity to intone it, since we were so dominant. Simon, the brilliant 880 yards and mile runner, was disqualified from the under-sixteen years mile for crossing out of his track too early. Pog O'Gallagher was already standing in his lane for the start of the open mile when Dinny McGahan approached him and was seen reasoning with him. We all know what the discourse was: 'You might get third or fourth, but young Simon can win it for us and break the record. Will you stand down?'

What an exquisite humiliation, to be asked to stand down for a younger, better athlete when you are already in the starting lanes! It was the harshest thing I ever saw Dinny do, but everything that worked was fair in sport.

Young Simon ran and won. *Black, black, rickety-rack* . . . Pog looked sick and clammy all the way back to Central railway. He would make up for it in later life by owning a string of pharmacies and liquor stores. On that afternoon, however, he shone with anguish.

Through these seasonal shifts, some change was occurring in me. I had once imagined myself in English classes at Sydney University, and perhaps later in Medicine or Law classes. Sydney University, however, as envisioned, now had less and less substance to it. It was an anaemic imagining.

Mangan sighed with a sense of deliverance as we fell to our books. The last time was past when he would be made to swim at Concord baths or field at deep fine leg or wear a coloured athletic singlet and run second last in some lowly race.

'The end of ignorant sporting,' he said, 'and the beginning of the true *vie spirituelle*.'

St Pat's did not teach French beyond the intermediate class, but Mangan continued to speak it with a stylishness which went unchallenged on the Western Line.

Sport had for now ended for me, but I had not retired as a spectator. I could still show that to me sport, art and religion were all part of the one rich continuum. On the first weekend of October, a few days shy of my seventeenth birthday, I took the train and bus to the Sydney Cricket Ground, carrying with me a volume of nineteenth-century poetry – because once Jimmy showed me the splendours of GMH I had grown a bit weak on the Romantics and now had to make up for it – and a small book on the Treaty of Locarno. I went on my own, since Matt had decided to spend the afternoon being tested in History – Ancient and Modern – by his father the Digger.

This was to be the supreme New South Wales day for Peter McInnes, the contest between all the boys schools' champions of New South Wales. Beyond this lay all the even more glittering days of Australian championships, Commonwealth Games, Olympics.

When I arrived at the Sydney Cricket Ground, there were not too many Strathfield uniforms on the concourse in front of the Sheridan Stand. In this bigger arena of contests, our sense of dominance had been reduced to scale. The competition would be hot. Peter won the 220 yards stylishly in a time which I forget. I remember only that it was an All Schools record. But everyone knew the great event would be the 100 yards.

Simon won the under-sixteen years 880 yards and mile – poor Pog well and truly eclipsed by now. There was no one on the Sheridan concourse to do *Black, black, rickety-rack* with though. The concrete space by the fence was full of boys from the best schools – Grammar and Saint Ignatius, and King's named in honour of the Monarch and identified by the para-miliary slouch-hat and uniform its boys wore. These were boys who were told in the classroom that they were Australia's inheritors, and probably were.

Yet Peter had put them all in second place. Men and women and boys went past, and what they all said was, 'Mustn't miss that 100 yards.'

I was tempted to enter into conversation with other boys there and offer them insights into Peter's training methods, to let them know off-handedly that I had trained with Peter and run for Canterbury-Bankstown with him. Fortunately, I resisted. The star sprinters came out at last in their sloppy joes, most of them barefoot on the concrete, holding their spikes. Peter wore his white ankle socks, a fashion I had imitated, hoping the cotton would give me an extra tenth of a second. You could see the journalists and commentators up in the sports booths in the M. A. Noble Stand – a battery of fixed binoculars all trained on McInnes. All the other finalists could run 10 or 10.1 seconds on their best day. Peter had yards on them. Only if he started appallingly could he be beaten. But I had seen Dinny running him through his starts every afternoon on the oval. A nasal *On your mark,*

Get set, and *Go! Go!* was actually a clap of Dinny's hands, and Peter was well gone down his lane before the sound of Dinny's hands reached me.

'Good, good, good,' the Christian Brother would cry after Peter. 'Ah . . . come back, come back.'

There was not a poor start in McInnes.

I took up a position on the fence ten yards from the finish line. Crowded in by other, faintly sweaty uniforms which had no tribal connection with Peter.

A lovely start. Faster than at the clapping of hands by Brother Dinny McGahan. By fifty yards, the crowd was beginning to laugh indulgently at the gap which had opened between Peter and the rest. He was not abnormally tall but his stride astounded the onlookers. Ten yards of daylight, as he crossed the finish, sat between him and some other normal sprinter running second. Yet I saw that at the line, something snapped at once in him. A fragile chord that connected his upper and lower body broke right then. This fracture drove him sideways, and when he straightened he could barely put his foot to ground and he began to stagger about with a broken, broken gait.

People in the stand, influential parents who had never heard of Homebush, stood up. Twenty thousand with their heads cocked at that angle of inquiry.

His medial ligament had snapped beyond any hope of being repaired. Today he could have been restored, could have taken only a season off. If the technology had existed, he would have been ready in time for the 1954 Commonwealth Games, the 1956 Olympics which Melbourne would ultimately acquire.

He was as much an inevitable Olympian as Mangan was a monk, and before our eyes, he had perished by the cruellest, un-chosen mischance. He was away from school only a few days and came back the same fellow but with a faint limp. After all, he had to get his study done for the Leaving Certificate. Of course, the fact that it was a life sentence was not fully known to him then, but that it was a substantial verdict did not alter him.

'A bit sore, Mick,' he would say to me, when I asked, which I probably did too frequently.

But I had been *there*, had seen it. The last great hope of Australian sprinting, better than Hec Hogan. He had run the 100 yards that Saturday afternoon in 9.6 seconds, and all the sporting commentators were weeping. He could have challenged Hogan, and would within a year certainly have beaten him. Ferrety little Hec would run third in the Olympic 100 metres of 1956. Pete would have beaten him and still have been good enough to take a medal at the Mexico Olympics in 1968, and in an utterly changed world, share the platform with the two Black Power signalling athletes from America.

Soon Australians would become too worldly and understand the size of the earth and know that they could not train on cow-paddocks and beat all comers. Peter was the best, lost hope of the era of innocence, and he came unstrung on a Saturday afternoon on a rough track at the Sydney Cricket Ground.

We could not get over our astonishment – particularly Matt and I who discussed it. This was the first instance of someone in our generation who stood so close to immortality that all of us could see or sense the aura. And yet it had all died in an instant.

'Too bloody fast for his own good maybe,' my father said, since Peter McInnes came under the category of sport and was one of the topics that was safe for us to converse on. Speed overwhelming the human framework! 'You've got to bring a sprinter along gradually,' he said. And no one could argue with that. It was the sort of bush wisdom prevalent in his barefoot sprinting childhood.

In any case, we knew at last and very clearly that glory could be denied. If Peter needn't win the Australian sprint championship, then Matt need not be admitted to Sydney University, and I need not become a poet who held hands with Curran.

VIII

I recovered from that as I did from most things: I called in at the Frawleys' kindly hearth. One thing seemed definite barring death: Rose was going to become a Dominican nun and wear their brown and white habit. The name Margaret already earmarked for her. She had that glory chest too, just like a girl going to be married, and into it she was stacking bed linen with her initials, pillowcases likewise, and the linen shifts and bloomers which nuns wore. She would hold some of them up to the light and say, 'Would I remind someone of Ava Gardner in these?'

Gentle Mrs Frawley said to me on one of those afternoons, 'Did the girls tell you Mother Concordia is dying?'

I must have frowned, because Mrs Frawley remarked that the old nun had had a good life. Concordia was the woman who had intimidated with a white chalk line all us six-year-old piddlers at St Martha's Convent. Death seemed in one sense a likely proposition – Concordia had seemed old ten years ago, when she urged us not to cause the Virgin Mary to blush.

'We're in the nuns' chapel hours on end praying for her,' said Rose, as if she did not see herself as a nun yet, the nuns being still *them*.

I thought of Curran, lean and olive, reciting the Sorrowful Mysteries in the wood-panelled chapel at Santa Sabina.

The mention of so austere a figure as Concordia of course by indirect paths reminded me that I was close to the time limit of pretending to be a potential priest. All the funkholes out of that destiny seemed to be guarded by arguments and ideas sharp as razors already unsheathed, and put in place by everyone from Father Byrne to the Cardinal.

For example: 'I've decided to go to university first.'

'*Yes, but many a vocation is lost that way.*'

'I've decided I don't have a vocation.'

'*Yes, but how can you tell until you've tested it?*'

Could I manage to say, 'But I like girls too much. One in particular'?

Or equally impossible, 'I had a revelation during Sunday Mass. God *revealed* that he had other plans for me.'

I was painted into the piety corner as certainly as Mother Concordia was herself cornered by nature and piety on the tall bier of her bed in the Dominican Convent. But I wasn't going. I couldn't go. It would have to be said.

The next morning I practised breaking the news to Matt.

'I've just about decided against going into the priesthood,' I told him.

He put his head on the side in his intelligent, tolerant manner, in a way which sometimes made me believe that he saw through all the posturing.

'There's always time afterwards,' he said with the hopeful, upward intonations which were his nature. This was a time of year when Dinny McGahan was letting the two of us sit outdoors on the verandah to go through our Pass subjects. We studied long hours, so that there was always time for a little desultory conversation. Even as Matt and I walked home we were still quizzing each other on Modern History or Shakespeare's soliloquies.

Coming back to Mattie's little bungalow on one of those first afternoons of knowing about Mother Concordia and her impending death, I saw Curran and her well-dressed mother walking together down

Shortland Avenue. Past the little suburban gardens they walked like two equals, intently discussing something. Bernadette Curran even wore her maroon Dominican Convent gloves, and Mrs Curran's gloves were white. They were two women dressed not so much to represent motherhood or daughterhood, but an impenetrable sisterhood. What they talked of was unguessable but, you couldn't doubt, marvellous. It occurred to me that whatever was going on there, my mother had been deprived of it in her two-boy, all-male family.

I told Matt, 'There goes Mrs Curran and Bernadette. They're dolled-up exquisitely!'

Matt gave a half chuckle. 'That must be pretty exciting for you, Tom,' he murmured.

I gave him a small nudge on the upper arm. But what they spoke of, the Curran women, transcended our chirping and banter. It had crux, it had weight.

Calling in at the Frawleys yet again, a household in which because of Mrs Frawley's kindness, Mr Frawley's serious purposes and the Frawley girls' genial mockery I felt appreciated, I found out what the Curran women had been discussing.

It was to do with Concordia, the matriarch of the Order. Like Mother Margaret, she had not borne earthly children. Yet this fact made all of them – the Frawleys, the Currans and all the rest – her children. In batteries, her daughters, class by class, girls small and large, in their impeccable maroon, had entered the Dominican chapel to pray for her deliverance or happy death. The Leaving Certificate girls were asked to come and go to the chapel only at their leisure, but come and go they did. A hush hung over their futures. Some may have even felt a pulse of an ambition to achieve in the end a death as notable, as reverberating as that of Concordia. Such a departure from the normal suburban or bush deaths of grandfathers and grandmothers!

The prefects of Santa Sabina were, I heard, admitted in a bunch into the large convent parlour, where Concordia's deathbed had been moved to allow for room for visitors. They saw the brave, rugged, sculpted face of Concordia, still cowled in the Order's regulation clothing for the sickbed at this supremest moment. They saw her lowered lids, and the effort of the discourse she pursued with God on earth's furthest up-jut, on land's end.

This was a death from an ancient and baroque tradition. Had there been what the Frawleys called 'some mad girl', some girl, that is, who was a temperamental echo of the mad boy I was, she might have been overly influenced, morbidly fascinated, inflamed by divine ambitions. But Curran was sensible, had no time – as I knew – for exorbitant responses. She should have come out safe from the visit to Concordia.

The full and potent magic of the death of the great Irish matriarch had not yet, however, been unleashed.

Imagine a room where the Honours English and History girls are at their desks, preparing for the coming public examination, when a messenger enters, a younger nun, and whispers to Curran. Mother Concordia wants to see Curran on her own. Walking out of the study, does Curran – who looks so settled in all life's circumstances – feel unsettled to be chosen to share some of Concordia's last seconds? She must not be totally at ease with such an excessive act of graciousness.

Here at last drama has found a way to penetrate Curran's matter-of-fact, no-nonsense, *Aussie* advance towards the greatness everyone agrees will mark her later life.

She approaches the sickroom where only the last watchers remain, the most senior nuns who have shared table and cloister with Concordia for years and who are now easing her on her way. Monsignor Loane is long gone from the bedside, with the canisters of holy oil with which he has anointed Concordia in the sacrament called Extreme Unction. Two nuns rise from their knees and take Curran by the elbow, bringing her forward to the deathbed. One of them touches Mother Concordia's shoulder. The old nun half opens her eyes. She tears her gaze away from Yahweh's long enough to say, 'Bernadette, I call upon you to become a Dominican nun and take my name, *Concordia*. I will pray for you and support you in the Presence of God.'

I still wonder if as Bernadette left the deathbed (and indeed the old nun would die overnight, eased of the question of the inheritance of her name) any nun said to her, 'Think closely about this. A command from Concordia is not necessarily a command from God!'

It had been after Concordia had made her severe bequest to Curran that I saw the Curran women speaking so earnestly on their way home and mentioned it to Matt.

It is wrong to surmise the decision was made for her by Concordia's deathbed edict. Sensible and democratic Curran was not so readily deprived of will as all that. But it must have had an effect in some scales of decision, and it seems she made the decision pretty quickly afterwards. She did not trumpet it though – I heard about it not from her lips. I had gone home with Matt to his house in Shortland Avenue, and his mother offered us tea and told us.

'Wow,' said Matt. 'What'll you do now, Mick?' Did he mean, how to top that? Or how to deal with it? I sat in a vacuum, my hands prickling. As soon as I could I left. It was as if this were a war, but all the maidens, not all the young men, were about to vanish. I walked bemused to the Frawley house in Broughton Road, and everyone was home except Mr Frawley the wiry grouper. Rose Frawley had answered the door with a half-smile.

'Have you heard the news?' all three women were asking. 'What will you do?' asked Rose. 'Join the Foreign Legion?'

She of course was delighted that she would have a sister, a Strathfield girl, a Santa Sabina girl, her own head prefect and 'brain', with her in the novitiate.

We discussed it. I felt a constraint over my heart, sharp edges against my ribs. The Oxford University Press Edition of GMH. I knew I did not need that discomfort any more. I took it out of my breast pocket and absent-mindedly slid it into my schoolbag.

The younger, gentler Frawley girl, Denise, cried, 'Did you see what Mick just did?'

Rose said, 'Sick of strung rhythm, are we?'

'Sprung rhythm,' I told her without any passion.

I got home and my mother did not notice merely the phantom shape of GMH in the grey serge coat she looked after so arduously. She had met Mrs Frawley outside Cutcliffe's Pharmacy in Rochester Street and had been told.

'This shouldn't have any influence on what you decide,' she told me.

When my father came home from his store in Granville, he said the same thing. 'Just because everyone else is volunteering it doesn't bloody mean you have to.'

He knew whereof he spoke. He had been a volunteer in his day, and had not been fully happy in the service.

What was worst for me was that I could tell that whatever Curran was renouncing in the name of the Deity and Concordia it was not me. No messages or hints had been sent. There was no chance of a last hand-hold.

Nonetheless, amongst the quicksilver shifts of sentiment occurring to me, there now grew a desire to be associated with such a brave drama. Curran's sincere choice put the question to me in a lasting way the Cardinal had not been able to. On the one hand the sublime path. On the other hand, the chance of a normal university degree and a little double-fronted brick cottage in a suburban street. GMH had been a priest in his cell and had sung like an angel in his chains.

There were references of pure and sublime love as well: Eloise and Abelard, St Francis and St Clare. And then there was the other, Australian example – Father Tenison-Woods and Mother Mary MacKillop. MacKillop the seraphically handsome woman, and Julian Tenison-Woods a priest like GMH, but a famed geologist rather than a poet. Mother Mary MacKillop had founded the Sisters of St Joseph, who lived in poverty and taught poor children in the Australian colonies. She spread her Order right through the world, so that she constituted an early Australian success story. I had seen Tenison-Woods' works in the library of the Brothers' house – *History of the Discovery and Exploration of Australia,* Volumes I and II, *Fish and Fisheries of New South Wales* and *Geological Observations in South Australia.* He quarrelled with Mother MacKillop, yet enthused her to found an Order and at the same time had an heroic sense of Australia's ancient geology. They – Tenison-Woods, elegant Brit, former *Times* journalist, and MacKillop, colonial girl – had once been photographed side by side, and made a remarkable pair. Mother MacKillop's piercing, enormous eyes. No fainting mystic. A good, practical woman. Like Curran in that. Could there be some possible similar and future alliance between Curran and myself?

The following Sunday the Currans had us all up to their little brick house at Strathfield for an afternoon tea. It was a kind of celebration and farewell. I did not take my GMH, what was the point? As we drank the tea and ate the *Women's Weekly*'s best sponge cake – it was still an era where women felt ashamed to serve cake from a cake shop – Curran did not make much of her decision, although Rose Frawley kept talking about it excitedly. She still remarked continuously on the fact she and Bernadette Curran would be Dominican novices together. I began to see that this blustery, open-faced girl-woman had been genuinely and pathetically scared of the tests in front of her, amongst novices she had never seen before. Now she would be able to look across the choir stalls to a known face.

Either Matt or Larkin the agnostic said, 'Which one of you will be Mother Superior first?' and we saw Mr Curran hide his face and turn his shoulder, which began to shudder. A shamed silence fell over everyone, and Mrs Curran went and laid a hand on his arm.

In that second I knew that I was going too. The sense of seeing the rituals from the *inside*, the way GMH had, overtook me again, but now it did not fill me with terror. It was in part a matter of crazily knowing that grief could not be avoided, and this grief displayed by the Curran parents was purposeful and noble. In the Currans' house at tea the richly-coloured skeins of motivation – a yearning for GMH's God, a desire to serve, a desire to instruct, a taste for drama, a preference for fleshless love, an exaltation in the Latin rites. I would never be bored by them, I knew. I would never listen surreptitiously in the confessional, between penitents, to the Saturday races.

So I walked home with Matt and Mangan knowing I would go. How the decision chastened, calmed and yet exhilarated me. I said nothing though, no longer a braggard. For a time I would imitate the style of the Currans and keep my decision secret. It struck me delightfully that I would have no bad news to announce to the Cardinal or Father Byrne, but I wondered how my father would take it.

At last on an ordinary Tuesday morning at school, I told Matt. He turned to me with his face on its normal questing angle. A morning in October, the month

I would turn seventeen. The wattle was out in vivid bloom
and air was beginning to take on what the Romantic
poets would have called a Lethean weight in preparation
for the usual hot and humid Australian Christmas. We
were reading Pass History on the verandah outside Fifth
Year Blue, in pleasant shade.

'Secular or monastic?' asked Matt. What sort of priest
would I be. Parish or in the cloister like Mangan.

'I'm going into Springwood,' I told him.

'Good,' he said. 'So we'll see you every Christmas.'

Whereas Mangan would disappear for life. I would
serve in a parish and go to Rugby League games. I
wouldn't be on a par with Mangan. I would never be a
Trappist who kept custody of the tongue and spoke only
on Christmas Day or in the extremest emergency. I would
keep the more normal monastic silences of the diocesan
seminaries at Springwood and Manly. But again, who
said that a diocesan priest couldn't write like GMH if
he chose?

I said, 'I'm sorry, Matt. It means I won't be beside
you at university.'

There was a little expulsion of breath and a faint
reddening of his skin. 'You couldn't be anyhow, doing
Law or Medicine.'

'I would possibly have done Arts first.' Would publish
poetry, become renowned, and not have had to go any
further.

He said quietly, 'They won't let me go anyhow. They've
got ordinances that forbid it.' He knew the world was
fortified with edicts aimed to keep him on the edge of
life. 'But I'll be fine anyhow if they *do* let me go.'

Neither of us feared that study companions for Matt
would be lacking amongst those young men and women
who were not frightened of his blindness.

'It's a good thing, Mick,' he told me. 'If it doesn't work,
you can always come out and go to university anyhow.'

But my absolutist temperament didn't like people saying that. Having decided to become a seminarian, I would not be the sort of seminarian who *left*.

That afternoon, in the little flat by the railway line, I broke it to my mother. 'I'm sorry,' I told her. 'But I'm not just playing around with the idea any more.'

She wept but said that she was in favour of anything which made me happy. This had always been the pattern – firmness, ambition for her children, but finally she was an encourager and indulger of unexpected directions they might take. This last and climactic time she went down to visit my father labouring with his tomatoes and onions at the bottom of the garden, and I watched her talking to him, and he shaking his head.

How I appreciate that fellow at the bottom of the back yard now. I have learnt from experience at many a bar and over many a dinner since that he was a robust drinking man, but he could not afford to drink at all during those years, even though he came from a tribe whose lives did not seem to have been at all shortened by drink. He possessed that taste for fashion which his negligent child lacked. He preferred good clothes and highly polished shoes and tailor-made cigarettes. But he had to heel-and-sole his shoes himself, and he had to smoke the world's thinnest roll-your-owns to enable us to go to St Pat's and get the glimmering of what people call *ideas above our station*.

Through the squat Irish mother who had raised him as the last of nine children, the last beloved son, he retained a passionate though ambiguous relationship with the Church. He knew that if your son was *called*, you had to cop it sweet – there was nothing else to be done.

At tea that night he made some remarks about 'throwing away your education'. And it was then, to keep him happy, that I fell back on Matt's line.

'Don't worry. If it doesn't turn out to be right, I'll come straight out and go to university.'

My mother spoke to him over days, and gradually he began to take some whimsical pride in having a son a potential priest. One day I asked him if he wanted to walk up to the school at Strathfield and play some tennis with me. We ran around the court chasing tennis balls until he was red-faced. A vigorous fellow though, I could see. Standing up with a retrieved ball in his hand, he said, 'Do you think I'll get a discount in bloody purgatory? For having a son a sky pilot?'

That's what they called ministers of religion in the bush town he grew up in, and in the RAAF in Egypt during the war. *Sky pilots*. He could not understand the honour which, as sky pilot, I intended to bring on the family name. The literary as well as the ecclesiastical honour.

One night though, cutting away at his well-done meat, he returned to an earlier theme. 'I hope this isn't some bloody reaction to that Bernadette Curran deciding to take the veil.'

I was innocently sure it wasn't.

Slowly the news got up and down our block in Loftus Crescent, Homebush, and was uttered as trains thundered through on the Western Line. Jimmy Smart, a great St Pat's batsman who lived at the corner, had a sister who married a Protestant, a genial man who worked for some department in the New South Wales Government. He was particularly amazed by the news. One afternoon when I met him on the street he gently asked me how I felt about never marrying. I forget what I told him.

Fellow Catholics by contrast began to look at me with new wonder and enquiry. Sometimes, outside Martha's on a Sunday, where Curran was a regular but not a relentlessly early visitor, the group of us – Mangan, the Frawley girls, Matt, Curran – would stand talking, and people who had heard of our various intentions would look on us with a new surmise. We had acquired an *esprit*. Dahdah was already in the seminary, Mangan of course was committed to be a monk according to the Spartan rules of St Bernard of Clairvaux, and one Frawley girl and Curran and I were bound for a great transformation from children to austere figures.

My parents were in the strange position of receiving greetings which were halfway between condolences and congratulations.

One afternoon immediately after my decision became known, while I sat with Matt on a brick fence by the Stockade, flush from making choices, I watched lean Larkin come up and bend towards me in a scholarly way he might have learned from his weekend drinking companions in the pubs around Sydney University.

'So you're really going to do it?' he asked.

I said of course I was.

'Why don't you join the police force, that might be easier?'

'Why do you say that?'

'Organized religion is a form of social control, and so is the police force. But you don't have to live in a monastery to be in the police force.'

'I don't understand what that means. *Social control?*' Had GMH been a sort of copper? Impossible!

'Religion is in place,' said Larkin, 'to distract the working class from what they haven't got.'

'That's old stuff,' said Matt. And indeed I had heard the *opium of the people* argument put by a number of folk, including Crespi the salesman. But I felt profoundly disturbed by this idea as uttered by Larkin; the accusation that all that motivated me was a desire to do this or that to the working and middle classes. He *knew* about GMH.

How easily it could have been argued if we'd been on some campus and a year older (by which time I might have agreed with him). But to have my vast choice depicted as the equivalent of becoming a junior constable turned the air sour.

'That's not what I'm going *in* for,' I told him.

'Oh, I know you see yourself as a clerical poet,' said Larkin. 'But look all around you. Do you perceive poetry?' He waved his hand round the surrounding streets – Hyde Brae, Merley, Francis. 'This is the stupor of real estate, and religion exists to protect it. To make the working class pleased to have nothing, and the middle class content with their sad little bungalows.'

'That's not it at all,' I said, but when I said it I thought of sleek Monsignor Loane.

Matt said nothing more. Did he have a grudging feeling of support for Larkin's position?

We went on arguing, but I was at a disadvantage from feeling betrayed by Larkin. He was speaking up for other, newer friends. He was not speaking up for the Celestials. My face burned. It was because I respected Larkin's intelligence, and wanted to be seen by its light as engaging in something Hopkinsian and inexpressible. I hated the way he depicted me.

Of course, I did not see that in his own way Larkin was a neophyte too. He was writing off property with the same lightness of touch with which I had written off sex.

❁❁❁❁❁

In the indefinite era leading to my decision, time had seemed to erode a grain at a time. Now, in this definite season, it evaporated, and I soon recovered from the intense but momentary hurt of my argument with Larkin.

In the midst of this period of slightly self-conscious wonderment, Matt and I had all at once to do the Leaving Certificate. We had been for some time ready, at least at the Pass level. We walked together, casually, from St Pat's to the state school, Homebush High, to do our Pass English. Homebush High had a good reputation and many future notables of Sydney and New South Wales would go there. It was of solid red brick and its catchment area was pretty much what St Pat's was, the west and south-west of Sydney. Its corridors were barer, slightly dustier, and of a different odour than St Pat's. This was the odour of secularism, the un-Gothic-ness of ordinary Australia. Having made the decision I had made, it didn't appeal to me. Yet I remember exactly its ambience now, forty years later, and its smell.

A special room had been set up for Matt, since he was making history, and an amanuensis – a young graduate of Sydney University appointed by the NSW Department of Education – had sat ready to write down Matt's answers.

At first it all went well. The Pass English Richard II and all the Romantic poets – no problem to such a Celestial, such an intimate of GMH, as I. Physics and Chemistry were a pleasant trot. Latin, which I would now most certainly need at Springwood and Manly, were equally accommodating – translating Catullus and Horace. Catullus's less obvious poems to his beloved and the verse addressed to his canary. In Pass History we regurgitated what Buster Clare had taught us to regurgitate, and found his bets on what would be on the paper quite accurate. I added in a little more from other reading I'd done in secret defiance. Just to make sure I got an A.

Late-night studying at Matt's, late-night studying at home. In the frenzy of preparation, my mother tells me, I appeared from the second bedroom which I shared with my brother Johnny, sleepwalking like Lady Macbeth.

But now the examinations got tougher. The General Maths paper was appalling – they were punishing us, Mangan and I told each other, for preferring to the sure firmament of algebra such useless things as imagery and the date of Mussolini's accession to power.

Writing for hours. St Pat's boys mixed in with Homebush High boys at desks in the examination hall, all united in the fragrance of paper and ink from the Government printery, writing our answers on the fragrant stationery of the New South Wales Government.

Soon the Pass process was over. Ten days. Matt, pleased with himself, was done. For me, Mangan, Larkin and others there were still the Honours examinations to be sat. Over at Strathfield High, Curran – the future Sister Concordia – would also sit down to the Honours exams.

I found that with both Honours English and History my knowledge was too particular. I wanted the examiners to honour GMH by asking a specific question about him, something which would allow me to expatiate on sprung rhythm. It was – like other years – more general than that.

'Poetry is image. Discuss.'

Instead of being what the yobbos who did Pass English thought – merely a rhyme. 'I'm a poet and don't know it.'

History too honoured the wide smear of knowledge rather than the particularities. I knew that Curran and her comprehensive knowledge would do well in all of this. At last I too had the exhilaration of handing over the last exam and walking away. No longer a schoolboy. In fact, by the time I reached the railway line between Homebush and Flemington, three blocks from Homebush High, already a putative adult.

⊗⊗⊗⊗⊗⊗

I had been told the Archdiocese was willing to offer me a scholarship to the seminary, but I had to raise some money to pay for other expenses, and had seen an advertisement in the *Catholic Weekly* from Pellegrini's, the Devotional Object Dealers and Booksellers, George Street, Sydney. They needed extra staff before Christmas and then through January, as the orders came in from various schools. I went in and applied. The thin manager had a calm, judicious, devout air which I supposed would permeate the entire company. I had heard that future seminarians got preference at Pellegrini's.

So I was put to work with a number of boys taken on specially for the season. We wrapped packages with missals and priests' breviaries and rosary beads and the latest works by Jacques Maritain or Frank Sheed, the cricket enthusiast and theologian, or his wife the theologian Maisy Ward. We boxed statuary and other objects – chalices, altarboy uniforms, surplices and stoles such as priests wore in the confessional. A label which would be attached with glue to the package had the name of the destination typed on it, some little bush convent, some parish priest in the sweltering Darling or Riverina districts.

The packing room lay out the back of the store in a Dickensian yard and up some ramshackle steps. Its supervisor came to me early on the first day and said, 'What sort of fucking knot is this?'

So it appeared that gravity of demeanour wasn't universal in Pellegrini's. To avoid further bullying by the man I observed other packers and saw how the classiest knots were tied, and soon became expert. After the year of hectic study and yearning I enjoyed the small challenges of packing.

The supervisor of the packing room, amongst the as-yet-unblessed and still purely commercial rosary beads, altar linen, surplices and devotional books, also exhorted us to watch out about string, we weren't rigging a bloody ship. And measure the paper carefully too. Fucking paper didn't grow on fucking trees. He was a nephew of a famous monsignor, and swore like a publican's nephew.

One afternoon he ordered me to go with him and a girl, a label typist from the office (a regular not a casual), down into the dank and humid basement to find some crates for shipping larger objects. The crates lay there amongst other bric-à-brac, and I dragged one of them out into the yard. When I returned for more, the supervisor was kissing the girl and fondling her breasts and she was resisting. I was shocked by what you could only call the naked grin on his face. Though it was theologically certain, as the supervisor's uncle would have told him, that mortal sin cut in when a man felt women's breasts, it wasn't dogma that worried me. It was the ugliness, sweatiness, goatishness.

I felt sorry for the girl too, who was shamed in front of me. She was fearful I'd spread gossip about this.

'What are you bloody looking at?' the supervisor asked me, as if in that fairly prudish age he could do what he was doing and not be looked at. A pained and dangerous smile took over his face. He was beginning to feel a bit silly, and threatened too. The girl straightened herself and left.

So this was sex – shame, awkwardness, reluctance, bullying and fear. Not such a big thing to miss out on. Better to be St Francis and St Clare.

Like the packing supervisor, however, I would soon enough make a fool of myself. It was towards Christmas, marked by high temperatures and high humidity. And yet Christmas must have counted for a great deal in the celebrations of Scottish, Irish and English settlers to the country, since it has always been robustly celebrated there, the heat bringing forth a profoundly-based, pri-mordial Australian hedonism.

Even in the devotional goods business, there was a tremendous overload of packing to be done to mark all the torrid bush and suburban Yules.

The normal after-hours way out of the packing department was via a door which locked shut behind you, down a stairwell and through another self-locking door into George Street. But we were told one Friday that if we were working very late, that was not the way to take, since the door at the head of the stairs had been somehow set to lock after us, and the door to the street would be unopenable from the inside. I don't know why this was so – perhaps management had got word of some proposed devotional goods heist. In any case, that night we were told to exit by a back laneway into Kent Street, and make our way around the back of all the businesses, and so by Liverpool Street to George, and then to the Town Hall underground station.

Leaving last after an overtime packing spree, I put out the lights, entered by habit the main building and exited the normal way, closing the door at the head of the stairs behind me and so finding myself trapped. I went down to the outer door, but it was immoveable. If I had broken the glass in that outer door, it would have left all the riches of Pellegrini's devotional warehouse open to plunder. I went back to the head of the stairs and contemplated staying the night. It was at this point that I ran out of stamina, and all the dark shadows of the manic exhilaration in which I'd spent the year struck me. A night is easy to wait through for a spiritual heir of GMH, but all at once the exhaustion from that feverish year seized me and I was unwilling to wait through this one. Using as a buffer a book I was reading – I believe it was Conan Doyle's *The White Company* – I punched a pane out in the upper door. So I let myself through into the body of Pellegrini's, and out by the laneway to Town Hall station and home.

I remember that this act of damage to property worried me greatly, and I lay awake thinking of excuses. What sort of person would the sage manager of Pellegrini's think I was?

The next day I turned up to work and absolutely nothing was said. Towards lunchtime, the packing supervisor came up and said, 'Are you bloody cut?'

I showed him the few grazes I had from the pane-breaking exercise.

'Next time, bloody sort it out in your head before you leave, will you?'

I bought plenty of Christmas presents (even a Graham Greene novel for my mother), and books and ties for my father. My mother laid special stress on its being my last at home. I would of course be back the following year, but she rightly knew I would be another kind of child by then.

That morning I made a brief visit to the Tierneys with a present for Matt, to the Frawleys with a gift for the Frawley girls. Mr Frawley was wistful. Rose would *not* be back next year, unless she fled the novitiate, which for some reason seemed unlikely. Though I had posted a fulsome Christmas card, I did not go to the Currans. Eloise and Abelard severely apart at Yuletide.

In the middle of January, just before Curran went away, we got our Leaving Certificate results. I had received two second class Honours and four As, even an A in the awful General Maths. This was what was called in those days a maximum pass, even though first class Honours would have been the *real* maximum. Matt had got three As and three Bs. The *Daily Mirror* came out to photograph him, and all of us gathered at his place – Larkin (who had done badly in Maths but got a first class Honours in History), Mangan (two second class, two As, two Bs), Dahdah come home on holidays, and myself.

The *Sydney Morning Herald* and the Frawleys had let me know that Curran had done dazzlingly. Like me she only received second class Honours in English, but first class in History. Rose had acquired a more pedestrian pass.

I remember a telegram from my father's cousin, Pat the lawyer, expressing amazement at how well I'd done. For some reason I still remember it with secret delight. It was soon followed by a letter from the Federal government informing me that I had won a scholarship to university. I could postpone it in case it was needed at a later date, of course. Mangan was also uselessly offered a scholarship.

Almost simultaneously with it came a letter from Sydney University addressed to Matt and his parents, indicating that the University Senate was powerless to alter the ordinances to allow Matt to undertake a degree. This decree fell like an axe across his triumph, but he seemed almost composed, as he had when Basher refused to let him run against his own age group. He and his parents had a valiant conviction of ultimate success and were sure the ordinance would be revoked in a year or two. (Their confidence in this was, I am happy to say, justified, even though Mr Tierney would not live to see his son graduate.)

My mother was already sewing my name to shirts and underwear for the seminary. My parents seemed almost happy and I had begun going to the bottom of the garden to chat directly with my father about radio programmes and Beethoven and poetry. 'Too bloody deep for me,' he told me jovially when I tried to explain sprung rhythm to him. 'Give me Banjo Paterson any day.'

I presumed that at the Mangan household, rather more disorganized than mine, similar preparations were afoot. I happened to run into Mangan one afternoon in Rochester Street and asked him again when it was that Trappist novices were supposed to turn up at the monastery in Victoria.

'Oh,' he said. 'I've been meaning to say something about that, but what with the exam results . . .'

'Yes?' I asked.

'The friars have actually recommended that a person should go to university first to learn how to deal with timetables. So I'm going off to university to study Arts for a year or so.'

I kept walking with him, but was pole-axed. We had been going to tread together back to an earlier, more mystical time, and now he was not going to keep stride with me. Rose Frawley and Bernadette Curran would go together, but I would be on my own.

'My parents would prefer it that way too,' said Mangan, who had rarely mentioned his parents before, given that he was a phenomenon, a bolt from the blue, a manifestation rather than someone's statistical child. I was astounded that he had listened to his parents. To what extent did I listen to mine, and to what extent flummoxed and harangued them?

I saw him go in the gate of his house, down the side to the disorganized Viney back yard. We were no longer troubadours. We weren't singing the same song.

I thought, So, I'll go alone. That was suitable. GMH had gone alone into the thickets of sprung rhythm and half-rhyme, tying his thick knots of imagery.

I stood alone in Rochester Street, ennobled by purpose.

❧❧❧❧

It was still the height of summer, the middle of January, and Sheffield Shield cricket was in full cry at the Sydney Cricket Ground. The turning of the year race carnivals my father went to and modestly wagered at had barely subsided when Mangan, Matt, the Frawleys, the Currans and myself travelled to Newcastle, to the new location of the Dominican novitiate Rose Frawley and Bernadette Curran were about to enter. It had previously been in the northern suburbs of Sydney but had now been moved to this grimmer locale. The Frawleys, mother and father, were in their best, and looked as transformed, as drenched in new light as people we know on a daily basis do when extraordinary circumstances descend on them. But I could tell, even from the viewpoint of the cock-eyed planet I occupied, that the Frawleys were more at ease with their daughter's destiny than were the Curran parents. I now know that the Currans would have preferred we were not there, in the parlour of the vast nineteenth-century Gothic novitiate, saying goodbye to their daughter. To Curran whose hand would go unheld *ad eternum*.

While the Frawleys looked proud, the Currans looked bereaved, and their bereavement – I wanted to say to them but thankfully didn't – would not be final. They too would enjoy the ultimate pride of the accommodation their daughter was making with the more real, the only important world.

The Currans it seemed were going to stay overnight with relatives in Newcastle, that fairly dour mining town part-way up the New South Wales coast, drab itself but named for a drabber town in Northumbria. I can imagine them now, how they might have stood by the convent walls the next day, Mr Curran inconsolable, looking at the bare brick with longing, wondering whether their daughter was thinking, 'Dear God, why am I here?'

'When do you go in?' Curran had been kind enough to ask me in the parlour at Newcastle as we waited for her and Rose to disappear utterly.

'Middle of next month,' I told her.

She smiled the smile which I now know could have got her into the movies.

'Some people have it easy,' she said.